IMAGES OF FAITH

IMAGES OF FAITH

*Spirituality of Women
in the Old Testament*

JUDETTE A. GALLARES, R.C.

ORBIS BOOKS

Maryknoll, New York 10545

The Catholic Foreign Mission Society of America (Maryknoll) recruits and trains people for overseas missionary service. Through Orbis Books, Maryknoll aims to foster the international dialogue that is essential to mission. The books published, however, reflect the opinions of their authors and are not meant to represent the official position of the society.

Copyright © 1992 by the Religious of the Cenacle, Philippines Region, 59 Nicanor Street, Loyola Heights, Quezon City 1108

Published by Orbis Books, Maryknoll, NY 10545
Manufactured in the United States of America

First published by Claretian Publications, U.P.P.O. Box 4, Diliman, Quezon City 1101 Philippines

Unless otherwise noted biblical citations are from the *Christian Community Bible.*
Copyright © 1991, Claretian Publications

Library of Congress Cataloging-in-Publication Data

Gallares, Judette A.
    Images of faith : spirituality of women in the Old Testament / Judette A. Gallares.
        p. cm.
    "First published by Claretian Publications . . . Quezon City, Philippines" — T.p. verso.
    Includes bibliographical references
    ISBN 0-88344-943-9
    1. Bible — Biography. 2. Women in the Bible — Religious life.
    3. Bible. O.T. — Biography. I. Title.
    BS575.G35   1994
    221.9'22 — dc20
    [B]   93-40764
                                                                    CIP

*For my fellow sisters in the Philippine Region
and to all Filipina Cenacle sisters the world over*

CONTENTS

PART TWO
PRAYERS BY WOMEN OF THE OLD TESTAMENT

PREFACE

An increasing number of books offering new insights into and feminist interpretations of the lives of biblical women are being written these days. This seems to indicate that there is not only a growing interest in the topic on the part of a greater number of people but also a growing awareness on the part of women theologians that they do have a theological voice to raise, and it is a voice that can no longer be muffled.

As I write this book, I am grateful to these women theologians and biblical scholars for their valuable contribution in expanding our consciousness and for blazing a trail for us so we may gain confidence in re-reading and re-interpreting Scriptures from our perspective. Many of their insights have found their way into the pages of this book and have sparked new thoughts and reflections.

Writing this book has also given me the privilege of getting to know the women of antiquity as if they were my personal friends. In my reflective moments I would find myself dialoguing with them and questioning them about their experiences as women during their time. I also tried to put myself in their place to imagine what life was like in their culture and situation. The process of recreating their stories in my mind and entering into their human struggles and spiritual yearnings has helped me understand not only my own interior struggles and spiritual longings but also those of the women of today.

Likewise, I wish to acknowledge and thank the many women who have told me their stories—those whom I have personally encountered and those I met only in my readings. In recounting their stories, I used fictitious names, except in two instances where the factual accounts I included in my reflections had already appeared in other publications. Although most of their names are fictitious, their stories are not.

I realize that what I am offering in this book is simply another voice — coming from Asia and the Third World — among the chorus of voices that are already being heard about women of the Bible and of today. But with this addition, I hope that more of us will come to appreciate not only the richness of our spiritual heritage but also the faith, sacrifices, and struggles of our foresisters in the light of who we have become as women of today and where we are now in our common journey.

In the completion of this book I owe a debt of gratitude to many people. I wish to thank all of them here, though I can mention the names of only a few. The first ones that come to mind are those of Fr. Alberto Rossa, C.M.F., director of Claretian Publications and Desiderio Ching, Claretian editor, who have been supportive of my projects and have encouraged me to put this volume together. I am also grateful to Sr. Malen Java, r.c., for reading the first section of this book and for offering helpful suggestions. My old school friend, Lorna Kalaw-Tirol, has been a great help in editing my manuscript and encouraging me to finish this project. I likewise thank Maria Delia C. Zamora for providing the artwork and Noel Morado and Miriam Cruz for their generous help with the final preparations for publication.

I owe special thanks to a community of fine women religious, the I.C.M. sisters of St. Theresa's College in Cebu, for their graciousness in allowing me to use their facilities. The sisters were my mentors in college when I studied in their school in Manila many years ago. I especially thank Sr. Perla Ramirez, I.C.M., for her kindness in letting me "pitch a tent" in her office so I could work on the computer there without having to worry about power interruptions.

Last but not least, I wish to acknowledge my own religious community, the Religious of the Cenacle, for the congregation's support in making this book a reality and for constantly challenging me to use my gifts and energies for the service of God's kingdom.

JUDETTE A. GALLARES, r.c.
Feast of St. Therese Couderc
26 September 1992

IMAGES OF FAITH

INTRODUCTION

The inspiration to write this book came to me as I read stories of struggles experienced by today's women and as I continued to encounter the faith stories of countless women in my ministry as retreat facilitator and spiritual companion. Many of them are poor. Yet in their poverty they exhibit an inner strength and a simple faith that remind me of the many women in the Bible, both named and unnamed, whose lives are woven so intricately within the pages of our sacred history. Traditionally, the portraits of the lives of most of these women are not seriously considered for their inherent significance. Some of these biblical women were never famous. Their stories were never highlighted by the church, as were those of Sarah, Deborah, Esther the queen, and Mary. Because of their socio-economic status and religious affiliation, they were not considered positive models for spirituality over the centuries. They were either pagan or poor, such as Hagar, the slave Sarah brought from Egypt who, because of her rebelliousness and disobedience to Sarah's wishes, has traditionally been considered a negative model for spirituality. The lack of recognition of who they are, together with biased interpretations in traditional biblical commentaries, has brought about this general negativism. However, with the re-reading of Scriptures from the third-world and feminist perspective, we can glean new insights from the lives of the not-too-famous women in the Bible. Nonetheless, whether they are named or unnamed, famous or unknown, their "positive" or "negative" roles in God's unfathomable plan of salvation can never be disputed. Many of them mirror a kind of spirituality that we need as a counterwitness to the androcentric, consumeristic, materialistic, and egotistic tendencies of our world today.

1

As we shall see in the lives of these women, they were receptive to the divine promptings; faithful to God; valiant in times of danger and death; persevering in the face of poverty, strife, and trials; vulnerable in their sorrows; sacrificial in their victim roles; and humble in their self-offering. The lives of these women of old wove designs of light or of darkness in the tapestry of our biblical past. Yet God planned that they would have a role, no matter how insignificant it might seem to be, in carrying out the divine message of salvation throughout all the ages. As I examine their lives more closely and reflect on their spiritual experiences, their message, their faith, and their relationship with God, I can't help but hear in their stories the experiences and struggles of many of our women today. As foreign contract workers; "hospitality" girls; domestic helpers; vegetable, fruit, or candle vendors; factory workers; professional "pray-ers"; scavengers; beggars; day-care workers; street people and loan collectors, they steadfastly cling to their humble and feeble faith that God will never abandon them and will someday lift them up from their miserable condition.

I believe that the women in the Bible have a lot to teach us about faith and prayer and spirituality. But so do the women of today who day and night cling to their faith in a seemingly absent and obscure God even as they live in sub-human, oppressive, and degrading conditions.

What can these women teach us about the meaning of faith and spirituality? What can they tell us of their relationship with God and about the relevance of prayer in our contemporary world? How are they challenging us in the authentic living of our faith? How can we learn to pray for them and with them? Let us therefore listen to the stories of the women of generations past and of today. In listening to them, let us identify with their doubts and struggles and allow our own life experiences and search for God to resonate with theirs.

In this book, I will attempt to let some of the women of antiquity and of today offer some answers to the above questions. This will be done primarily in the first section of the book, "Spirituality of Women in the Old Testament," where the main focus will be a discussion of the biblical character's experience of life, her faith, and her spirituality. Here I am using the word *spirituality* in connection with its roots in Hebrew, *ruah*, breath, spirit, life — something that comes from or belongs to one's depth that vivifies and animates. It belongs to guts, feelings, experience, and innermost thoughts. Thus the spirituality that we will be discussing is an integrated one where both mind and heart are involved in the living of one's faith. It is a spirituality that moves and informs a person to act on his or her faith every day.

In the first section of the book, I will develop the discussion on faith and spirituality in the following manner: First, in each chapter I will take a biblical character(s), relate her or their story through the pertinent passages in the Bible and discuss the possible meanings and interpretations of the Scripture passages based on my own re-reading of it and that of other contemporary women writers and theologians. This re-reading as a method of doing or constructing theology is done with an informed commitment to women's liberation and to human liberation in general.[1] This has to be done because the Bible with its heavily patriarchal context and androcentric language cannot be spontaneously reappropriated by women. Even male prophets "who were aware of oppression by rich urbanites or dominating empires were not similarly conscious of their own oppression of dependents—women and slaves—in the patriarchal family."[2] Thus a sensitive re-reading of Scripture seems urgent in the context of how religion and Scripture have been used and misused to justify and sanction the oppression and subjugation of women through all the ages. Such a re-reading is also appropriate at this juncture of our church's history, where inculturation of local churches is being encouraged and where greater emphasis is being placed on the liberating message of God's Word, especially for people who are experiencing all kinds of bondage. Author Elsa Tamez puts it well when she says:

> There are in the Bible re-workings of events originally grounded in particular meanings, events actualizing faith in situations of crisis reworked because their original impact had faded. They are re-read not with the intellectual curiosity to understand the past, but with the need to respond to life situations today. Our present . . . enters and

functions as filter, criterion, and light in the search for meaning in biblical texts.[3]

Hopefully each chapter will be a "historical re-reading of our foresisters for full humanhood and to reappropriate their victories and their defeats as our own submerged history."[4]

Secondly, I will discuss aspects of prayer and biblical spirituality that are being presented to us by the biblical character or characters. From the discussion, I will draw some insights on prayer and spirituality and possible ways of praying that hopefully will be applicable to us in our daily life.

Thirdly, I will parallel the biblical account with an account about contemporary women. I will include some of their stories—how they see or experience their situation of poverty and oppression as women and as victims, how they struggle in their faith, and how they experience God's presence or absence in their daily life and in this world.

Finally, at the end of each chapter I will suggest some ways of praying and reflecting with the women of old and of today. In doing so, it is my hope that those who will take this to heart will slowly come to feel their solidarity with the suffering and oppression of women all over the world.

The second section of this book will be devoted more specifically to prayers by women of the Old Testament. Here I will take a biblical character, give a description of who she is and the Scripture passages referring to her. Then I will either rephrase, paraphrase, or simply quote directly from the Bible the prayer attributed to the biblical character before offering some suggestions on how to pray with her. My main purpose in this section is not only to introduce the biblical characters to the reader but also to allow their prayers and faith to inspire and encourage us in our spiritual journey.

This book is not written for women only, although the title alone might naturally attract more women readers than men. I believe that there is much that men can gain from reading this. After all, part of the goal of every person's growth is the integration of one's polarities—the masculine and the feminine within the self. Thus, whether we are man or woman, rich or poor, slave or free, we are all inheritors of God's promise (Gal. 3:28).

PART I

SPIRITUALITY
OF WOMEN
IN THE
OLD TESTAMENT

1

HAGAR

The Oppressed Foreign Worker

In the patriarchal world of the Bible, to be a woman meant to be an inferior human being; to be a foreigner meant to have no legal rights and to be discriminated against like the widows and the orphans; and to be a slave meant to have neither freedom nor right to control one's destiny. Thus to be a woman, a foreigner, and a slave all at the same time was a triple tragedy. She was not only subject to discrimination but was also marginalized three times over. She was among the most humble, most afflicted, and most despised members of society.

This was the unfortunate lot of Hagar, Sarah's Egyptian handmaid and slave in Abraham's household. Her story in the Book of Genesis is overshadowed by the prominence given to Sarah's crucial role in Israel's history. Traditionally, biblical commentators have projected Hagar as a villain in the life of Sarah, interpreting her attitude to her mistress as insolent, disobedient, and arrogant. Most Bible studies would focus more on Abraham and Sarah and their roles in the foundation of Israel's faith. This particular bias has unconsciously programmed us to identify ourselves more with Sarah rather than with Hagar. According to Elsa Tamez, we do so for two reasons:

> First, because the stories are so constructed as to lead the reader to such identification, and because Sarah's role is crucial in the history of Israel. Second, because the story continually emphasizes the submission of the workers, and the attitude of Sarah towards Hagar appears quite natural.[1]

To get away from this traditional way of reading, Tamez suggests that "right at the beginning we must recognize these two elements, and consciously distance ourselves from them, in order to read the text, or perhaps reconstruct it, from the perspective of third world women."[2]

HAGAR'S STORY IN THE BIBLE

According to Scripture scholars, the following two accounts come from two sources—the Yahwist and the Elohist.[3] These passages seem to be two variations of one story. Since our interest is to get to know the character of Hagar and her situation, we shall read both accounts as one continuous story, mindful that each source would have its own bias.

Through the Eyes of the Yahwist (Genesis 16:1-16)

> [1] Sarai, Abram's wife, had not borne him a child, but she had an Egyptian servant named Hagar, [2] and she said to Abram, "Now, since Yahweh has kept me from having children, go to my servant; perhaps I shall have a child by her." Abram agreed to what Sarai said.
> [3] Abram had been in the land of Canaan ten years when Sarai, his wife, took Hagar, her Egyptian maid, and gave her to Abram her husband as wife. [4] He went in to Hagar and she became pregnant.
> When she was aware of this, she began to despise her mistress. [5] Sarai said to Abram, "May this injury done to

me be yours. I put my servant in your arms and now that she knows she is pregnant, I count for nothing in her eyes. Let Yahweh judge between me and you." ⁶ Abram said to Sarai, "Your servant is in your power; do with her as you please." Then Sarai treated her so badly that she ran away.

⁷ The angel of Yahweh found her near a spring in the wilderness ⁸ and said to her, "Hagar, servant of Sarai, where have you come from and where are you going?" She said, "I'm running away from Sarai, my mistress." ⁹ The angel of Yahweh said to her, "Go back to your mistress and humbly submit yourself to her." ¹⁰ The angel of Yahweh said to her, "I will so increase your descendants, that they will be too numerous to be counted." ¹¹ Then the angel of Yahweh said to her, "Now you are with child and you will have a son, and you shall name him Ishmael, for Yahweh has heard your distress. ¹² He shall be a wild ass of a man, his hand against everyone and everyone's hand against him, defiant towards all his brothers."

¹³ Hagar called upon Yahweh who spoke to her, and said, "You are a God who sees." ¹⁴ That is why this well is called the well of Lahai-roi. It is between Kadesh and Bered.

¹⁵ Hagar gave birth to a son and Abram called the child Hagar bore him, Ishmael. ¹⁶ Abram was eighty-six years old when Hagar gave birth to Ishmael.

Through the Eyes of the Elohist (Genesis 21:1-21)

The chapter begins with a narrative about Isaac's birth, the child of Sarah and Abraham in their old age (vv. 1-7), then continues with an account of Hagar's dismissal by Abraham in the following verses:

⁸ The child grew and on the day Isaac was weaned, Abraham held a great feast. ⁹ Sarah saw the child that Hagar, the Egyptian, had borne to Abraham, mocking her son ¹⁰ and she said to Abraham, "Send this slave girl and her son away; the child of this slave must not share the inheritance with my son, Isaac."

¹¹ This matter distressed Abraham because it concerned

his son, [12] but God said to him, "Don't be worried about the boy and your maidservant. Listen to Sarah and do whatever she says, because the race which is called by your name will spring from Isaac. [13] But from the son of your servant I will also form a nation, for he too is your offspring."

[14] Abraham rose early next morning and gave bread and a skin bag of water to Hagar. He put the child on her back and sent her away. She went off and wandered in the desert of Beersheba. [15] When there was no more water in the skin, she pushed the boy under one of the bushes, [16]and then went and sat down about a hundred yards away, for she thought, "I cannot bear to see my son die."

But as she sat there, the child began to wail. [17] God heard him and the Angel of God called to Hagar from heaven and said, "What is the matter, Hagar? Don't be afraid. God has heard the boy crying. [18] Get up, pick the boy up and hold him safely, for I will make him into a great nation." [19] God then opened her eyes and she saw a well of water. She went and filled the skin and gave the boy a drink.

[20] God was with the boy. He grew up and made his home in the wilderness and became an expert archer.

[21] He lived in the desert of Paran and his mother chose a wife for him from the land of Egypt.

A RE-READING OF THE STORY

The First Episode: Genesis 16:1-16

At first glance, we read through the eyes of the Yahwist in Genesis 16:1-16 a glimpse of the frustration and jealousy of Sarai, the insolence of Hagar, and the passivity of Abram. Perhaps if we look at it again and try to get behind the situation, we can discover nuances that will give us a new understanding of the characters' attitudes and behaviors.

First, let us look at Sarai's situation and how women were generally regarded in the ancient world at that time to understand Sarai's feelings and struggles within herself. Then let us look at slavery at that time in order to understand Hagar's situation and why Sarai gave her to Abram as a concubine or secondary wife (vv. 1-2).

Sarai is presented as barren and beyond child-bearing age. As a woman, she received her legal rights only through her husband. In a patriarchal society where everything is viewed from the masculine perspective, a man's wife is listed among his blessings, the riches of his household.[4] Consequently, if a woman remains unmarried or is widowed, she is automatically marginalized by society. Yet marriage has its own peculiar demands on the women—they are expected to provide descendants to their husbands. They are considered blessed by God only if they can bear children. Thus Sarai's sterility is seen as a curse, a humiliating condition that brings personal suffering not only to her but perhaps also to her husband, Abram, to whom God promised to make him a great nation and his name great (12:2). With Sarai's sterility, Abram perhaps began to wonder how God's promise would be fulfilled.

Sarai's disgrace prompts her to find ways to provide descendants for Abraham. She then decides to take matters into her own hands to be assured that Yahweh's promise of descendants would be fulfilled. She does this by resorting to a common law at that time allowing barren wives to give their slaves as concubines to their husbands that they might have descendants (v. 2).[5] In such cases the children of the slaves became the legitimate children of the master. Sarai's intention of giving Hagar to Abraham is clear, but its fulfillment is not going to be that smooth. Instead the intended solution to Sarai's predicament develops into a complicated situation. What was thought to be a simple and accepted arrangement becomes a source of psychological conflicts in Abram's household. Since she has taken matters into her own hands, Sarai's plan about Hagar seems to "blow up in her face." Perhaps this was God's way of "showing" that the promise would be fulfilled in God's way and time and not according to human machinations.

To have a greater understanding of this development, let us look at two factors that contribute to the complexity of the situation: the situation of slavery at that time and the status of a foreigner.

Throughout the period covered by the Old Testament and the New Testament, slavery was common. A person became a slave for one of the following reasons: by purchase, by capture in war, by birth (from a slave), as restitution, by having defaulted on debts, through selling oneself, and by abduction.[6] The slaves at that time were considered properties. They had no rights, although they were governed by some laws on slavery. Most of these laws favored the masters, however, rather than the slaves themselves. They were mostly in domestic service to wealthy families. Abram and Sarai were relatively affluent, having been blessed by God with flocks and herds of animals and other possessions. In other words, they could afford to have slaves. We do not know how they acquired Hagar, but it would be reasonable to think that they acquired her while they were in Egypt to escape the famine at Canaan (12:10). However, she could have been an *apiru*, which in ancient languages like Ugaritic was a term applied to marginal groups of people like bandits, mercenaries, the landless, the poor, etc. As an *apiru*, she could have sold herself into slavery because of extreme poverty.[7]

Whatever might have been the circumstances that led Hagar into slavery, it is clear in the text that she belonged to Sarai. She was Sarai's slave and as such was like a powerless object that was under her mistress's control. Sarai saw Hagar as a solution to her problem. But by being given to Abram, Hagar attained a new status of concubine or secondary wife. "It is certainly understandable that a servant who now shares the master's bed may assume a certain equality to, or even superiority over, the barren wife."[8] Suddenly Hagar realized the meaning of her pregnancy and decided not to give her own son over to her mistress. Sarai was distressed by the failure of her plan, viewing Hagar's decision as an insult to her. Her barrenness and inability to provide a descendant for her husband became a more painful reality.

But did Hagar really "despise her mistress" (16:4b), or was this simply Sarai's interpretation of Hagar's attitude? Here the narrator's bias is also clear. He does not allow Hagar to speak for herself, for after all slaves do not have such a privilege. We only have Sarai's words to rely on and those of the narrator. Hagar's silence may be contrasted with Sarai's determination to do something about her infertility.[9] But even without Hagar's own words, we can construe from her actions a change in her self-perception. No longer a slave but a secondary wife, she begins to perceive herself as a person with a right to make decisions, and as the pregnant wife of her master, involved with him in the completion of God's promise.[10] This change in self-perception threatens Sarai, for it lowers her position and self-esteem. Hagar, in perceiving her own conception of a child, acquires a new vision of Sarai—a vision that removes the hierarchical blinders that culture has placed on her.[11] Paradoxically, Sarai herself was responsible for exalting the slave's status.

Meanwhile, we can feel the "gathering storm" within Sarai. In her anger, envy, and jealousy, she confronts Abram with her predicament and obliges him to do something about the situation (v. 5). In one translation of the Bible, Sarai even blames Abram when she says to him: "You are responsible for this outrage against me. I myself gave my maid to your embrace, but ever since she became aware of her pregnancy, she has been looking on me with disdain . . ." (NAB). This translation seems to imply that Abram perhaps showed more love and attention to Hagar, who was carrying his longed-for offspring. It would be reasonable to presume Hagar's natural reaction to this—it made her feel more important than the legal wife.

Perhaps for Abram this was the fulfillment of God's promise to him in chapter 12, the answer to his questions. But would it be acceptable to have foreign blood obscure his family lineage? Family codes at that time specified that such an arrangement was acceptable, but it was not exactly ideal for Sarai and Abram nor for the Hebrew culture.[12] This put Hagar, a stranger in the land of Canaan, at another great disadvantage. As a foreigner, she was always subject to discrimination and was always counted among the least important, like the widows, the orphans, and the poor. Even if her status were raised as her master's concubine, it did not change the reality that she was a foreigner. Something had to be done to solve this dilemma. Sarai provides us the answer by citing a law that is clearly on her side. The law imposes a penalty on slaves who, on becoming concubines, try to gain special status with the legal wife. The penalty specifies that they be returned to their former status as slaves.[13] Perhaps Hagar was ignorant of that law or, knowing about it, may have chosen to suffer the consequences of the law in order to keep her own child. It would be understandable if Hagar did choose to keep her child, for to a poor woman like her, a child is life's only blessing. To the poor, their children are their only blessing, a consolation and help in times of difficulty and companions in their old age.

To resolve this conflict, Abram takes the path of least resistance and decides to comply with the law by returning Hagar to Sarai (v. 6) rather than suffer the wrath of a jealous and angry wife. Speaking for the first time in the scene, he chooses not to exercise power and remains passive.[14] By doing so, he chooses to go against Hagar's feelings and the interests of his own son who, according to the law, deserves to have the rights of a first-born son. Like an object, Hagar is powerless against a powerful woman who has the law on her side. She is again a slave. This time she will suffer greater oppression in the hands of her mistress. If we were to imagine such a tension-filled atmosphere, it would be understandable that Sarai would rather get rid of Hagar than have a hated slave in their household. But the law at this point is on the side of the demoted slave. It specifies that "the wife has the right to send her back to slavery, but not to sell her to others."[15] She's stuck with Hagar. The law is not of great help to Hagar either, who has to contend with Sarai's hatred and cruelty. It would have been better had Hagar been sold to another master. The conflict between the two women only worsens. Sarai oppresses her more than ever and takes out her venom on the slave while seemingly sparing her husband from her wrath. Hagar, instead of submitting herself further to such cruelty, decides to flee and die in the desert. In her new consciousness as a person, making such a decision seems better than allowing herself to be subjected endlessly to her mistress's humiliations and inhumanity.

A stranger in a foreign land who has experienced great oppression always longs for the warmth of home. Perhaps this was Hagar's thought when she fled south to escape her mistress's harsh treatment. She was apparently on her way back to Egypt when she was met near a spring in the wilderness by the messenger of Yahweh who called her by her name and asked her where she was going (vv. 7-8). This is the first time in the narrative that a character speaks to Hagar and uses her name, thus acknowledging her personhood.[16] By including the reference of the "spring," the narrator indicates that although Hagar is in barren territory, she is at a life-giving source.[17] But the angel's message is like a "two-edged sword" piercing Hagar's heart. It contains both comforting and disturbing news. The angel's greeting makes her speak for the first time in the narrative, and her words will reveal to us the great suffering she could hardly endure from her response—"I'm running away from Sarai, my mistress" (v. 8b). After Hagar's response the angel begins with the disturbing news—"Go back to your mistress and humbly submit yourself to her" (v. 9b). As if to soften the blow of the first message, God's messenger immediately gives her the comforting news—"I will so increase your descendants, that they will be too numerous to be counted" (v. 10). The angel's words of assurance resonated with the promise given to Abram (cf. 12:2). Hagar is the only woman in the Bible ever to receive this promise, yet it lacks the covenant context that is so crucial to the founding patriarchs.[18] As Abram would become the father of "a multitude of nations," so would Hagar become the mother of many. As the first woman to receive an annunciation, this Egyptian slave became the prototype of special mothers in Israel for whom the unborn child signifies not just comfort but also suffering.[19] Hagar's son would be named Ishmael, meaning "God hears," for Yahweh did hear her cry and came to her aid. This same God many generations later would respond in the same way as the cries of the poor and oppressed Israelites in Egypt would rise to the heavens.

This section of Hagar's story ends with a description of Ishmael according to the etiological meaning of his name. He is the son of a proud and rebellious mother and becomes the ancestor of the desert tribes, known for their wild, free spirit and warlike nature (v. 12).[20]

The final verses (vv. 13-16) of this episode seem to have some connection between the etiological name given to the "spring" or "well" where Hagar had her encounter with God (v. 7) and

Hagar's naming of Yahweh as the "God of vision" or the "God who sees." It ends with Hagar giving birth to a son and Abram calling the child Ishmael, the name given earlier by Yahweh's messenger to Hagar (v. 11). Abram was eighty-six years old when this happened.

In the intervening fourteen years, much takes place in the lives of Abram and Sarai. In chapters 17 and 18, God specifies that the promise to Abram of a son will come from the birth of the aged Sarai. Their names are changed to Abraham and Sarah as an indication of God's plan to make Abram "the father of a multitude of nations" (17:5).

The Second Episode: Genesis 21:1-19

The first seven verses describe the birth of Isaac, the child of promise of Abraham and Sarah. The Elohist narrative of Isaac's birth is a duplication of the story of the expulsion of Hagar and Ishmael found in the Yahwist version in chapter 16. But there are significant differences. In this episode, complicating elements have been added, such as the expansion of the cast of characters in the persons of Abraham's two sons by different mothers — Ishmael and Isaac. The behavior of the characters also undergoes some changes. Sarah is presented as speaking less but accomplishing more; Abraham is not speaking but resisting; God is intervening directly; and Hagar is suffering increasingly.[21] In the Yahwist narrative, the emphasis is on Hagar's arrogance, not on Sarah's jealousy. In this episode, it is Sarah's jealousy, not Hagar's arrogance, that prompts Sarah to demand that Abraham expel the two.[22] However, the focus of this episode is not on Isaac, the child of promise, but on the consequences of Isaac's appearance on the scene to Hagar and Ishmael.

The scene begins with the occasion for the unfolding of the story — the day of Isaac's weaning, an event that calls for a big celebration. Here Abraham, the proud father, holds a great feast (21:8). The setting triggers in Sarah a whole complex of emotions and reactions that will lead to the expulsion of Hagar and Ishmael.

Now Sarah saw the son of Hagar the Egyptian, whom she had borne to Abraham, playing (21:9, RSV).

In another translation, the verse reads:

Sarah saw the child that Hagar, the Egyptian, had borne
to Abraham, mocking her son . . . (21:9).

Whatever translation one might prefer, this particular verse has
prompted different interpretations from Scripture scholars and
laypersons alike. Some studies[23] have stated the range of meanings given to this single verse based on the Greek Bible translation which says that Ishmael was "playing with Isaac." Some
meanings given are "Ishmael physically abusing Isaac" and "the
social equality implied between the two children was unacceptable to Sarah." When the phrase "with Isaac" is omitted, as in
the RSV translation, other interpretations follow, such as "Ishmael was masturbating" or "his joyous demeanor aroused Sarah's maternal jealousy." Other Scripture scholars contend that
nothing in the text suggests Ishmael abusing Isaac; it is a theme
deduced by readers trying to soften the actions of Sarah.[24]

Whatever meaning we might choose to attach to the verse,
we can be certain of this: Sarah is now contented because the
son of her womb has been weaned after coming through the
risks of infant death and has now entered a new stage of development. As such, Ishmael's presence would only complicate
matters for her son, Isaac, in terms of inheritance. She is pre-
sumably well aware of the law that the adopted child of a slave,
which Ishmael is, is equal to the child of the legal wife insofar
as inheritance is concerned. Jealousy and fear for her son's
future lead her to demand that Abraham expel the two. But
Abraham's reaction here is quite surprising as compared to the
Yahwist version, where he remained passive. The Elohist narrator says: "This matter distressed Abraham because it concerned his son" (21:11). As a father, he seems to be concerned
only with his son, not with Hagar. He gives in to Sarah's demand
to let Hagar and Ishmael go only after God tells him to do so
and when God assures him that Ishmael will be the father of a
great nation (vv. 12-13). Here God seems to be on the side of
the oppressor, even sanctioning Abraham's breaking of existing
laws. It also appears that the "powerful" can dispense with the
law if it does not serve their purpose. What law are they dis-

pensing with? The ruling law in that region did not allow a child born of a slave to be thrown out of the house and recognized the right of election of the child of the legal wife, but not of inheritance.[25] The law added that "no one can change that legislation, not even the mistress of the house . . ."[26] Was this perhaps the reason Abraham at first reacted to Sarah's demand and that God had to intervene before he could act in Sarah's favor? Therefore, based on the existing laws, Sarah could never throw the child of Hagar out. But she did, with Abraham executing the job for her.

In verses 14-21 the Elohist paints for us a poignant scene of the departure of Hagar and Ishmael. Abraham bids them goodbye with a heavy heart, giving provisions to Hagar—some bread and a skin bag of water—as they head in the direction of the desert. The picture is of a mother whose young child is being placed on her back by a sad father.[27] What were Hagar's feelings? This time she is not leaving by choice; she is simply doing what her powerful masters have decreed. Nor is she rebelling against the injustice of it. Leaving is to her a better option than enduring the injustice she has continually experienced for many years in Abraham's household. In leaving, she hopes to enjoy greater liberty. Now that she is Ishmael's sole parent, neither Abraham nor Sarah can claim any right to him.[28] Perhaps God allowed this to happen to ensure a better future for Hagar and Ishmael than if they had remained in Abraham's household.

Hostility follows Hagar. This time she experiences not human hostility but the hostility of nature—the scorching heat of the desert sun, the coldness of the night, and the harshness of the territory. The narrator's arresting description of Hagar on this journey evokes feelings of pity for her and her son, and anger at the powerful couple who forced her out:

> She went off and wandered in the desert of Beersheba. When there was no more water in the skin, she pushed the boy under one of the bushes, and then went and sat down about a hundred yards away, for she thought, "I cannot bear to see my son die" (vv. 14c-15a).

Hagar's suffering worsens when her provisions run out. Compared to her first experience in the desert where she found herself near a spring, this time she is in the wilderness with a container of water that soon becomes empty.[29] To emphasize her predicament, the narrator describes the place where she leaves her child—"under one of the bushes." Helpless and desperate, she wants to shield her child from the scorching heat and to give him a little comfort as he lies dying under the bush. In doing so, she is also giving herself some comfort by shielding herself from the painful sight of watching her only child die. But as she sits a few yards away, her child begins to wail (v. 15b). Ishmael's cry pierces the skies and evokes a response from God.

The depth of Hagar's suffering is the point when God will again appear to her. The narrator shows that God, like Hagar, cannot stand the sight of her dying child. At first glance, it would seem that God is concerned only for the child and not for Hagar because the narrator states that God heard the boy's voice and not Hagar's.[30] Jeansonne explains this succinctly:

> However, Hagar is crying because her child is dying; by hearing the cry of the boy, God is responding to the imminent death of the child, which, of course, causes Hagar to weep. Moreover, the messenger specifically addresses Hagar. Unlike her earlier encounter, this time she is addressed by her own name, without the appositive "servant of Sarah." The message to Hagar is one of consolation. She is told neither to be troubled nor to fear.[31]

The angel tells her to rise from her desolation, giving her a new sense of hope when she is told to pick up the boy and hold him safely, for God intends to make him into a great nation (v. 18). The same promise that was given her during her first encounter with God is repeated here to remind Hagar that the divine promise would never be reneged. To cast away any doubts in Hagar's mind, God "opened her eyes and she saw a well of water. She went and filled the skin and gave the boy a drink" (21:19). Life overcomes death. The possibility of a new tomorrow dawns with their new lease on life.

The last two verses of this episode complete the story of Hagar and Ishmael. It begins with an assurance of God's providence on Ishmael and where he will make his home: "God was with the boy. He grew up and made his home in the wilderness and became an expert archer" (21:20). In an exercise of her new-found freedom from the shackles of slavery, Hagar goes to her own descendants in her choice of a wife for Ishmael. In her last act, she guarantees that these descendants will be Egyptians, of her own race and culture.[32] There may be those who will not be impressed by God's promise to Hagar to make Ishmael the father of a great nation, considering that God later transferred that promise to Abraham (21:13), but for a powerless and poor woman of her culture, it is a striking reward.[33]

IMAGES AND CHALLENGES OF FAITH

Besides symbolizing the oppressed and the exploited, the homeless and the rejected, the powerless and the helpless, the accused and the despised, Hagar is a crucial figure in biblical theology from the third-world and women's perspective. Unimportant in the eyes of the patriarchal church, Hagar in many ways continues to shape and challenge our Christian faith. What challenges does she pose to us? What expressions of faith and ways of praying can we learn through her life and through the experiences of today's Hagars?

From our re-reading of her story, we saw that she is the first person in the Bible to have been privileged to experience a divine encounter and the only person who dares to name God.[34] She was even visited by God's messenger twice! Feminist theologians contend that within the historical memories of Israel, she is the first woman mentioned in the Bible to have borne a child (excluding the accounts found in the first eleven chapters of Genesis, which are considered part of Israel's prehistory). Trible expounds on this point:

> This conception and birth make her an extraordinary figure in the story of faith: the first woman to hear an annunciation, the only one to receive a divine promise of descendants, and the first to weep for her dying child. Truly Hagar the Egyptian is the prototype of not only special but all mothers in Israel.[35]

Poor and insignificant though she was, she deserves to be given stature in biblical faith, for she "foreshadows Israel's pilgrimage of faith through contrast" as she flees from suffering and bondage through the desert.[36] The Israelites many generations later would likewise flee from their bondage into the desert. At closer look we can glean from her story several images of faith.

The desert, because of its barrenness and dryness, has always been considered a land cursed by God. The ancient people considered it a place where evil spirits and other malevolent beasts dwell. Yet the sands of the desert run through all of salvation history and the whole tradition of three great religions: Judaism, Islam, and Christianity. Women and men of these traditions, with faith and no faith, had either been led there or had fled there for personal or religious reasons. There they came face to face with themselves and with God. There they had to come to terms with their own nothingness and with the reality of their deluded and denatured self and their desecrated and dehumanized world. It was there that Moses encountered God and received his mission. It was also there that God led the Israelites to experience liberation from Egypt. It was there that God made a covenant with the Chosen People.

In the Christian tradition, Jesus was led there by the Holy Spirit to be tried and tempted by the devil and to prepare him for his mission and vocation. The early fathers and mothers of the desert also went there to come to terms with the forces of evil in themselves and in the world.

For the people of the Bible, the desert is both holy and terrible. It is the arena of trial and struggle, a place where the values of life are presented in clear, naked terms; a place where one has to take the initiative in favor of life; and a place where one discovers the existence of God and gets to know the power of divine compassion and providence. It is only in the desert, whether real or symbolic, that reality becomes recognizable and unambiguous.

Hagar fled to the desert twice. Twice she also encountered God's messenger. The first time was when she was pregnant with Ishmael as she fled from her cruel mistress (16:7), the second time when she was banished from Abraham's household and at the point of dying from thirst (21:16). On both occasions, God saved her and blessed her, even if she did not know there was a God. Here we see that God's manifestation in the Bible is contained ultimately in the experience of salvation from death to life. Hagar was the first to receive such divine manifestation. From her experience, we come to know God's mysterious and marvelous ways, and from her divine encounter we come to know God's desire to convert all human hearts.

What is this process of conversion through which God is leading us based on Hagar's two experiences of divine manifestation in the desert? We have already seen that when one encounters the Divine in the desert, one inevitably comes to know oneself and one's values in clear, stark reality.

In Hagar's first encounter, we can begin to identify the movements of conversion and prayer. The *first movement* (16:7) in the process is the "desert" experience — a necessary disposition to encounter God. Like Hagar, we need to be confronted with our own nothingness and our need for salvation. In our nothingness and silence, we learn to listen and hear another voice, a voice that is not human but divine.

This disposition prepares us for the *second movement* (16:8), which is the experience of dialogue with the Divine. Prayer begins to happen when a person learns to speak in freedom and with honesty of heart in response to God's promptings. Before this encounter, Hagar was never allowed to speak for herself. In the story itself we get a glimpse of her and her predicament only through the voice of the narrator. Abram and Sarai never called her by name. For the ancient people, a name is not simply a conventional designation but rather an expression of a being's place in the universe. The fact that the narrator referred to Hagar only as Sarai's maid or slave impresses upon us the condition of a slave — one who does not have a rightful place in society. But in the desert, in her first encounter with the Divine, God's messenger calls her by name. Here she is allowed to speak for the first time as she responds to the angel's greeting.

As she learns to speak and enters into dialogue with the Divine, she is led to a confrontation with herself and with the whole of her life. This is the *third movement* (16:8) in the process of conversion and prayer: to begin claiming one's own experi-

ence of how one has lived one's life. Here the angel asks Hagar:
"Where do you come from and where are you going?" The first
part of the question, "where do you come from," reflects her
entire past, while the second part, "where are you going,"
involves her future and the direction of her life.[37] I guess we can
never change ourselves for the better unless we look at our life
with great honesty and begin to claim our painful past. God
cannot heal our wounds unless we open our hearts to divine
mercy and healing. Hagar, too, had to learn to lay bare her whole
life before the Divine and to allow God to show her the direction
that she needed to follow. Only then could God continue to
show her the path she had to take. And so she responds with
honesty and sadness of heart: "I'm running away from Sarai, my
mistress." This single statement tells us everything about her
feelings with no elaboration from her.

Awareness of our need to change is necessary for conversion.
But awareness alone is not enough. We must be willing to take
the necessary action toward our own growth. This is the *fourth
movement* of the process of prayer and conversion: to be willing
to engage in action or to change one's ways based on God's
direction (16:9). For Hagar, the path was to return first to Abraham's household and to her mistress. As a human being, Hagar
also had her share of human frailty. I suppose that even without
her meaning to, she did hurt her mistress by her seeming arrogance. Perhaps God did not want her to flee from her oppressors
without her learning to face them first as a person, even if they
might not have treated her as one. A person can meet the challenge to grow emotionally and psychologically only by not fleeing
from oneself but by squarely facing the other in whose presence
one sees a shadow of oneself. So the disturbing news announced
by God's messenger urges Hagar to return to her mistress and
submit herself humbly to Sarai (16:9), not because her mistress's
tyranny is just but because she, too, as a human being with her
own faults and frailty, needs to be freed from her own arrogance
and inner bondage. "What God wants is that she and her child
should be saved, and at the moment, the only way to accomplish
that is not in the desert, but by returning to the house of Abraham."[38] She has to allow herself to continue experiencing bondage in Abram's household for her unborn child's sake, that he

might have a chance to survive and claim his right as Abram's firstborn.[39]

From what kind of bondage does God want to free us? Like Hagar, we experience human bondage on three levels. Her bondage was clearly *physical* because as a slave she was restricted in her movements and was forced to work without recompense. Isn't this the kind of bondage that most poor people are subjected to? We see in her physical bondage the poor, oppressed worker; the old "shut-ins"; the illegal aliens; the pregnant, unmarried girl; the homeless; the destitute; the squatter; the abandoned wife with many children; and the people of the Third World who are forever in economic bondage because of their indebtedness to affluent nations.

Hagar's bondage was also *psychological* because she was valued only for her usefulness and as an object that could be dispensed with. She was unwanted, merely tolerated, and dehumanized. In her we see not only our own psychological bondage but that of the exploited prostitute, the "other" woman, the deported alien, the indigent relying on handouts from the power structures, the street children and runaway youths, and all those who are not treated with respect and dignity as human beings.

Finally, Hagar's bondage was *spiritual* because she was hated, not loved, and because she was left without hope. This is also the picture of all the Hagars of today who, in their desolation and experience of injustice and hate, question whether there is really a God, or who in their ignorance do not know that there is a God.

Thus, because of our experience of bondage, God wants to free us, sometimes through a painful path. One commentator says that sometimes this painful message is God's word for so many people who suffer injustice in our society: for girls who, in a liberal, class-conscious society, must accept humiliating tasks in order not to die of hunger with their parents; for the young people who, after a university education, realize that except for a select few, modern society needs only sweepers and laborers.[40]

Finally, we can discern whether or not we are truly following the right path only through our experience of God's reassuring presence. This is the *fifth movement* in the process of prayer and conversion (16:10-12). For Hagar, this divine reassurance comes in the form of a promise, an annunciation similar to that of Mary in the New Testament. The angel's "annunciation" to Hagar contains elements that belong to the classic form of "annunciation." These are the following: the announcement (look, you have conceived); the birth (and you will bear a son); the name of the child (whom you will call Ishmael); the significance of the name (because Yahweh has heard your affliction); and the future of the son (he will be a wild-ass of a man, his hand against all, and the hand of all against him, and he will place his tent in front of all his brothers).[41]

In this first encounter with the Divine, Hagar gives us an image of God as she names the deity "the God who sees" or "the God of vision." This is the *final movement* in the prayer process — the naming of God (16:13-14)! She is the first person in the Bible to ever dare to do so.[42] In giving God a name, Hagar fixes in her heart the image she has of God: a God who continually sees the suffering of the oppressed even if they do not call on God. God enables the oppressed to see that there are other possibilities in life, as God showed Hagar the source of water to quench her thirst. Hagar was even surprised that God should be interested in her. She exclaims: "Can it be that I have come to see the one who sees me?" (16:13, JB). She, the poor Egyptian slave, experienced the divine manifestation because God wished to point out that the oppressed are also God's children and co-creators of history; God does not allow them to perish in the desert without leaving a trace.[43] The poor and the oppressed are also human beings, with human dignity and a right to be part of our world and history.

The second faith-image that comes to us in our reading and re-reading of Hagar's second encounter with God is that of *a desolate mother's "faith."* According to our usual understanding of faith based on our Jewish and Christian perspectives, it may be perceived that Hagar does not have the kind of "faith" that we know. But she does. Let us look more closely at her experience of the second divine encounter and identify the various movements of faith and prayer inherent in that encounter.

Hagar's second encounter happens in chapter 21. Here, Ishmael is already on the scene, making it very poignant. Both are in danger of dying of thirst, for their supply of water has run out. Compared to her first encounter with God, where the Divine initiates the dialogue, here it is the child's wailing that evokes a divine response. Although the text itself does not specifically say that Hagar too was crying, we can easily imagine that she was because the previous verse is full of pathos: "she pushed the boy under one of the bushes, and then went and sat down about a hundred yards away, for she thought, 'I cannot bear to see my son die'" (21:15). As Hagar cries desolately, God's messenger begins to speak to her: "What is the matter, Hagar? Don't be afraid" (21:17b). God does not confront her with her past or her future, only the present, which is full of desperation and hopelessness.[44] In this prayer movement, God again invites her to speak from her heart—the heart as the place of prayer and the center of who we are before God. Like the first encounter, prayer or dialogue with God begins only when a person can speak from one's heart with great honesty. But here Hagar does not speak in words but in silence—a silence that speaks louder than any human speech. God immediately comforts her with courage, enabling her to pick up her crying child and hold him safely. Valiantly she has to take the role of both mother and father until the child grows to maturity and fulfills his role in life: "for I will make him into a great nation" (21:18b). Hope is restored in her. She revives from her desperation and is able to see a new possibility of life for herself and for her son: "God then opened her eyes and she saw a well of water. She went and filled the skin and gave the boy a drink" (21:19). Ishmael grew up and made something of his life in accordance with the "annunciation."

From our discussion of Hagar's second encounter with God, we can identify three distinct movements of prayer and faith: The *first movement* is the need to express where we are psychologically and spiritually—to express in words or in silence what is truly in our heart. In the text, Hagar's silence and tears tell everything. The *second movement* is to have courage and not to give in to our negative feelings—our fears and our discouragements in life. When we allow ourselves to sit in silence in our desolation and desperation, the silence enables us to see God's light and thus to hope again. As Hagar sat "about a hundred yards away" from her dying son, she had some time to sit with her depression. This enabled her to hear God and to receive God's courage and enlightenment. The *third movement* is to act according to God's enlightenment. Even if the action involved would entail some difficulties, the knowledge that God is there to guide us along the way strengthens our faith. Only faith in God's word and guidance can enable us to go on with our life knowing that the divine assurance or reassurance is there. God indeed is a God of consolation, as we saw in Hagar's second divine encounter and as the Book of Lamentations reminds us:

> Good is the Lord to one who waits for [God], to the
>   soul
>   that seeks [God];
> It is good to hope in silence
>   for the saving help of the Lord (3:25-26).

TODAY'S HAGAR

Reading and re-reading Hagar's story and her encounters with God bring to our mind images and scenes of oppression suffered by countless women in our world today. Here are some images which I have encountered in my ministry and in the unfolding of events in our society. One image is a familiar scene: a domestic servant is thrown out of the house by her mistress because she bears a child by her master whom she was powerless to resist. In this scenario, the servant is taken as an object and thrown out as an object.

Such was Brenda's situation when she ended up begging at the church steps after being thrown out of her master's house. Orphaned at sixteen, she decided to come to the city to seek employment as a housemaid. The only other person left in her family was an elder brother who had never been heard from since he left home several years before. Her other known relatives in her hometown were too poor to take her in. Besides, she had heard that life was better in the city. She knew someone from her hometown who was working in the city as a housemaid and who could help her get employed.

When she got there, her friend's employers allowed her to stay in their house until their former business partner could come from another city to employ her in his household. Brenda felt hopeful that this middle-aged, childless couple would be willing to take her in. She did not mind going with them to another island and city for as long as her future was assured. But no sooner had she settled in her new job when her master began to make sexual advances toward her. Powerless and afraid to resist him, she gave in. In the beginning her mistress treated her kindly, but when she found out Brenda was with child by her husband, she summarily dismissed her while the husband was away on a business trip.

What hurt Brenda deeply was that her mistress did not try to find out her side of the story. She was heartlessly thrown out of the house and told never to show her face again to her nor to her husband.

Homeless and confused, she wandered the city. A stranger in a new city, she had no one to approach for help. At one point she thought of throwing herself in front of speeding vehicles in order to end her misery, but she thought of the child in her womb. What future could she give the child, destitute, ignorant and helpless as she was? Wandering aimlessly for days, she found herself near a church. Hungry, tired, and broken, she sat at the church steps begging for food until Feling, an old widow and devoted church worker, took pity on her. Brenda cried as she unburdened herself to this kind woman. Feling, who lived in a squatter area, decided to take her in temporarily.

Brenda continued to stay with Feling even after she gave birth to a son. Feling had told her she could stay for as long as she wanted. Brenda feels that she has finally found a home and the mother that she has longed for. Grateful to God for her newborn son and for Feling, she has promised to take care of her benefactor in her old age.

Like Hagar, Brenda experienced God's visitation at a point in her life when she was down and out. A woman mercilessly threw her out, but another woman compassionately took her in.

But not all end up blessed like Brenda. In Pakistan alone, thousands of girls working as domestic helpers in rich or middle-class homes end up abused and exploited by the men of these houses. When a male child is born, it often happens that the man takes him and gives him full rights as his son, but a female child is often suffocated and thrown into the garbage to be eaten by dogs. Hagar's figure continues to haunt us all over the world in the lives of many who still are awaiting God's visitation.

Another image that comes to my consciousness is that of Asian women flocking to the oil-rich Arab countries by the thousands to work as maids.[45] Like the *apirus* of our ancient past, many have chosen to become virtual slaves in a foreign country to seek economic relief from their poverty back home. In their stories we hear the quiet desperation they endure for the sake of the families whose lives and future depend so much on their income. A great number of them find themselves assaulted sexually and abused physically and psychologically by their Arab employers.[46]

Some are fortunate to leave their abusive employers to seek better jobs somewhere or to return home. But others are not. Such is the case of two women named Lorna and Linda. Their stories were retold by a woman columnist in a Philippine newspaper.[47] I read the column when I was just beginning to write this chapter. I saw in their gripping stories a parallelism with Hagar's plight and therefore decided to include them in my reflections.

These are their stories as retold by journalist M. Ceres P. Doyo. First, let us listen to Lorna's plight:

> Lorna Laraquel, a Filipina maid, is facing trial for stabbing to death her mistress, a princess of the Kuwaiti royal clan, inside a flat in a suburb in Egypt. According to the story, the maid was driven to kill her employer because of the threats she had been subjected to. Apparently Lorna's employer did not believe her protestation of innocence — that she had not stolen but was in fact returning those U.S. dollars she had found — and kept badgering the poor maid. ... And because Lorna rushed to return it she was suspected of being a thief. We're presuming of course that Lorna's story is true.
>
> True or not, thief or not, Lorna did not deserve the treatment she claimed she got after the incident. Lorna's

employer could have right away dismissed her if she no longer deserved their trust. Why subject her to threats of "cutting off her tongue, cauterizing her eyes and throwing her onto an uninhabited isle when they returned to Kuwait"? Worse, Lorna supposedly heard her mistress telling someone on the phone to take Lorna back to Kuwait and there carry out the punishment.

Upon hearing that, Lorna grabbed a kitchen knife and lunged at the princess who had been threatening her. Lorna succeeded in killing her mistress but not herself as she had intended because a neighbor rushed in and grabbed the knife from her.

Imagine yourself a maid, with little education, with problems back home, working in a foreign land, suffering from culture shock, alone and working with strange people with strange habits. . . . And being constantly threatened with torture and mutilation. Would you not go mad? Would you not develop homicidal feelings or murderous tendencies?

We don't know much about Lorna's background, but we can presume that she is poor, otherwise she would not have ventured to leave her own family and country. Like Hagar, she chose to endure discrimination both as a foreign domestic worker and as a woman in a culture and religion known for its bias against women and whose laws have been known to impose upon the guilty harsh and heartless penalties such as death by beheading.

We can almost imagine that if found guilty, Lorna would probably suffer the same fate as "Linda," another Filipino maid who was executed a year or so ago for a similar crime. Columnist Doyo cites Linda's story in connection with Lorna's case and quotes excerpts of Linda's farewell letter to her children and husband back home to give us a glimpse of the continuing struggles of many oppressed foreign domestic workers today. Like Lorna, Linda killed her employer's son because he had ceaselessly subjected her to mental torture. Excerpts from her letter reveal her motive for committing the crime and her poignant feelings as she says good-bye to her family. To her children, she writes (translated from the Filipino language):

My children, the only thing I can say to you is be good and take care of your younger sibling if I should be brought home dead. . . . Just bury me in your grandfather's grave. The reason why I killed my employer's child is because they are no good. I have suffered hunger for six months here. Another reason is every day my employer's child has threatened to kill me. . . . Every hour I am told I am to be killed which is why my mind has no peace.

Sounding fully aware of her fate, she wrote a separate letter to her husband in which she repeated the reason for her crime but added that she did it in order to get him (her tormentor) first before he could succeed in getting her.

Reading her letter and knowing the torment she was being subjected to, we feel human pity and understanding for her deed. We don't know how Linda's last moments were spent and what thoughts and feelings were in her mind and heart as she faced her executioner. All we can surmise from her letter is the absence of fear in her as she confronted her fate. Did she think of calling on God? Or did she feel that there was no God at all? Where did she get her courage as she faced death? We will never be privileged to know the answers to these questions, for they are now buried with her. But as her story lingers in our consciousness, I hope that she, like all the other Hagars of yesterday, today, and tomorrow, will continue to challenge and shape not only our faith but also our faith response to the situation and structures of oppression in our world.

PRAYING WITH HAGAR

Suggestions for Prayer and Reflection

• Read and re-read Hagar's story in the light of contemporary issues and images.

• Then reflect on the following questions: Do I see any connection between Hagar's story and the lives of today's Hagars? What are my feelings and inner movements?

(Pause for reflection)

• *Prayer of Solidarity.* Continue in silence by praying for today's Hagars as you slowly read the following scriptural verses[48] (use one or both):

> (a) Yet it was our infirmities that [she] bore,
>   our sufferings that [she] endured.
> Though [she] was harshly treated, [she] submitted
>   and opened not [her] mouth . . .
> (Isa. 53:4,7a, NAB)

> (b) I tell myself my future is lost,
>   all that I hoped for from the Lord.
> The thought of my homeless poverty
>   is wormwood and gall;
> Remembering it over and over
>   leaves my soul downcast within me.
> But I will call this to mind,
>   as my reason to have hope:
>
> The favors of the Lord are not exhausted,
>   [God's] mercies are not spent;
> They are renewed each morning,
>   so great is [God's] faithfulness.
> My portion is the Lord, says my soul,
>   therefore will I hope in [God]
> Good is the Lord to one who waits for [God],
>   to the soul that seeks [God];
> It is good to hope in silence
>   for the saving help of the Lord.
> (Lam. 3:18-26, NAB)

• *Prayer in Action.* Concretize your prayer by engaging in some action that would address any kind of oppression or discrimination. Here are some suggestions:

— Reflect on how you treat the helpers in your own home. Try to rid yourself of unjust or oppressive ways (if any).

— Offer temporary refuge to anyone who has been unjustly

dismissed by her employer. Help her find justice.
— Raise the dignity of the poor and oppressed by treating them as persons.

Involve yourself in some concrete action that would address any kind of oppression or discrimination in your home, community, and nation.

2

RAHAB

The Faithful Prostitute

Prostitution is known as the "oldest profession" in the civilized world. In ancient biblical times, it was referred to as harlotry. The entire Fertile Crescent with which the Israelites found themselves in contact practiced this "profession" in the form of either simple harlotry (a woman prostituting her body for money), or religious prostitution (male and female prostitutes participated in licentious rites and orgies for the deification of the productive forces of nature).[1]

However, women and girls rarely became professional harlots by choice. Oftentimes they were forced into it by poverty, or they were chosen by pagan priests for cult prostitution, or they were simply sold off to male customers through "white slavery."

In ancient biblical times, harlots solicited patrons by sitting veiled at crossroads or gateways, or they conducted houses of prostitution and lived in them. Such was Rahab. Perhaps she began as a simple harlot who sat at the gateway of Jericho to earn her living in exchange for the fleeting pleasure she could offer the men of her time, and later on she conducted a house

of prostitution herself. We don't know much about her child-
hood and background except that when she appears in the Book
of Joshua she is one known to be conducting such a house. Her
place, located strategically just outside the walls of Jericho,
becomes the setting of her story in the Bible.

RAHAB'S STORY IN THE BIBLE

Her story begins at the time when Joshua (Moses' successor
and the one tasked to bring the Israelites into the Promised
Land) is preparing to conquer Canaan. This is the way her story
goes according to the Deuteronomic account:[2]

> [1]Joshua sent two spies secretly from Shittim with the fol-
> lowing order: "Go and look over the land well, especially
> the city of Jericho."
> The spies went and as soon as they came to Jericho, they
> went to the house of the prostitute named Rahab.[2] But
> someone told the king of Jericho: "Some Israelites have
> entered here tonight to spy on us." [3] So the king of Jericho
> sent word to Rahab: "Send those men out of your house
> because they came to spy on the land." [4]But the woman
> had hidden them, so she said: "It is true; they came to my
> house but I did not know where they came from. [5] And at
> nightfall, shortly before the city gates were to be closed,
> they went out. I do not know where they went, but hurry
> and you will surely overtake them." [6] The woman had hid-
> den them on the roof of the house, under the stalks of flax
> which she kept there.
> [7] The pursuers went to search for them by the road
> leading to the valley of the Jordan, and as they went out,
> the city gates closed.
> [8] Then the woman went up to where she had hidden the
> spies of Joshua, [9] and she said to them: "I know that Yah-
> weh, your God, has given this land to you; we are fright-
> ened and the inhabitants of the land tremble before you.
> [10] We know how Yahweh dried up the waters of the Red
> Sea to let you cross when you came out of Egypt. We know

what you did to the two kings of the Amorites who lived at the other side of the Jordan, to Sihon and Og, whom you destroyed by anathema.

[11] The news has frightened us, and everyone has lost courage because of you, for Yahweh, your God, is God in heaven above and he is on earth below.

[12] Now then, swear to me by Yahweh that just as I have been faithful to you, so shall you be towards my family,

[13] and respect the life of my father, mother, brothers and sisters, and all that belong to them."

[14] The men answered: "Provided that you do not reveal our intention, then we will pay back life for life when Yahweh hands over to us this land, and we will deal generously and faithfully with you."

[15] Then she let them down by a rope through the window, since her house was built into the city wall. [16] But she said to them: "Go through the mountains so that you do not meet those who pursue you. Remain in hiding for three days, until they return, and then you may go your way." [17] They answered: "See how we shall fulfill our oath. [18] When we enter this land, tie this scarlet cord as a sign on the window through which we have escaped. Bring into your house your father, mother, brothers and sisters, and all your relatives. [19] If any of them leaves the house, he shall be the one responsible for his death, and the guilt will not be ours. But if anyone who is with you is killed, then may the punishment for his death come upon us. [20] However, be careful not to reveal our plan. If you do, then we are freed from the oath we have sworn." [21] Rahab said to them: "So be it." And after she had sent them off, she tied the scarlet cord to the window (Josh. 2:1-21).

The spies did as Rahab had instructed them, and when they finally reached Joshua, they gave him an account of their mission and all that had transpired. In the intervening chapters, we read of how Joshua crossed the Jordan and prepared his people for their entry into the land Yahweh, their God, had promised their ancestors.

Then Rahab's story is picked up again at the conquest of

Jericho. Joshua is giving his last orders to his people, telling them to shout their battle cry for Yahweh and conquer the city. He specifically tells them to spare Rahab the prostitute and all those who may be with her in her house because of the aid she has given to his spies (6:17,22). The story thus concludes:

> [22] Two men had been sent to explore Jericho (and upon entering the city, were hidden by a prostitute). Then Joshua said to them: "Go into the house of the prostitute and bring her out with all her family as you had sworn to her."
>
> [23] These young men then brought out the woman named Rahab, her father, her mother, her brothers and sisters with all her relatives to safety outside the camp of Israel.
>
> [24] Afterwards, they burned the city and all that was in it. They saved only the silver, gold and the vessels of bronze and iron which they put with the precious things in the Sanctuary of Yahweh. [25] Joshua saved the prostitute and all her family, and she lived in Israel, because she had kept the spies sent by Joshua (Josh. 6:22-25).

A RE-READING OF RAHAB'S STORY

A Deuteronomic Tale: Joshua 2:1-21

The story reads like a war novel in which women are placed on the scene to play a part in an espionage plot against the enemy, thus spicing up the narrative with some excitement and suspense. What is the writer's intention in including this story in the book? What significance does it have to Israel's faith and ours?

Most Scripture scholars agree that the story of Rahab and the spies in its original form was probably an etiological tale, that is, a narrative that explains something by giving the story of its origin.[3] The story is included to explain the survival of the Canaanite family in the midst of the Israelites after the conquest of the Promised Land. However, like the patriarchal stories in the Book of Genesis, the central issues do not come from etiologies.⁴ Although such information enhances our understanding of God's Word, this will not be our main concern. Our intention here is to read the narrative as it is actually written from the perspective of a Canaanite female prostitute.

To put ourselves in Rahab's shoes, let us consider her situation as a woman, as a prostitute, and as a Canaanite. We have already seen in the previous chapter that the women in the ancient Near and Middle East ranked second in status to the men. Along with the children, the women were considered minors. Their influence remained restricted to their function as mothers. Thus, if they did not fulfill their expected role, their status was more diminished, like those who remained unmarried or who turned to harlotry. But the status of harlots was even lower. In general they were considered an underclass and, because of their life of immorality, unclean like the lepers. Consequently, they were looked down on, disdained, and avoided in broad daylight even by the womenfolk of better repute. In the secrecy of the night, however, men flocked to them to satisfy their lust. It would not be difficult to imagine that some, if not many, of the Israelite men were also involved in these secret affairs. That is why the Mosaic Law had to address this issue. To curb the evil influence of the Canaanite practices on the Israelites, the Mosaic Law strongly forbade harlotry among the Hebrews. If a betrothed Israelite woman or a priest's daughter was found to have prostituted herself while still in her father's house, the people would stone her to death for having committed an evil deed in Israel (Deut. 22:21). Like many laws existing at that time, this one was heavily biased against women, especially prostitutes. They were the ones penalized, while the men who used them for their own pleasure got away "scot-free."

Fortunately for Rahab, she was not an Israelite. Since the Canaanite religion used harlots or cult prostitutes for a form of religious service, Canaanite society was more tolerant of them. On the whole, however, harlots continued to be marginalized unless they belonged to a special religious caste that would offer their services to Canaanite priests or priestesses to deify the productive forces of nature through licentious rites and orgies.⁵ In such a case, they would be living in or near Baal's temple. Israel loathed much that was associated with the Canaanite religion and regarded Canaanite life and ways as abominable. Israel's literature urged the eradication of the Canaanite religion together with the Canaanite people (Deut. 20:16–18).

The fact that Rahab's house was located outside the city walls is an indication that she was not a cult prostitute but one who belonged to the marginalized group. Only the poor and those of ill repute lived outside the city walls or on the fringes of the city. However, the text seems to suggest that she was a harlot in the broader sense of the word, meaning a woman who kept a public house. Such houses would understandably be located outside the city walls because of the "shady" business going on inside. Paradoxically, as the story unfolds, the location of her house will work to her advantage and that of her family and kinsfolk.

Aside from the strategic location of her house[6] — it was built into the city wall (v. 15) — its structure also seems to have been useful to the spies. The upper story of the house was evidently higher than the city wall, thus enabling someone to look into the city itself through the window (2:15). So public was her place that someone saw Joshua's spies entering it that night. This was immediately reported to the king of Jericho who sent word to Rahab to surrender the two men (vv. 2–3). But she chose to defy the orders of the king. Instead she hid the spies and lied to the king's messengers, and when the pursuers were gone, she helped them escape by climbing down a rope from her window. In doing so, she was taking a big risk, assuming she was well aware of the existing laws that exacted heavy penalties on erring women. Based on the Hammurabi Code, one law specified that:

> If outlaws have congregated in the establishment of a woman wine seller and she has not arrested those outlaws and did not take them to the palace, that woman wine seller shall be put to death (Ham. Code 109).[7]

Public houses like the one Rahab was keeping most likely had wine for sale to the men who went there. Spies, being criminals and enemies of the state, were naturally considered outlaws. Thus the law would be applicable to Rahab. But like the rest of the poor and those of ill repute, she could easily take risks because she did not have much to lose.

We really don't know what the two spies told Rahab. Did they tell her the truth and the purpose of their mission, knowing that as a marginalized member of society she could easily be their ally? Or did they intimidate her, leaving her no option but to help them out? Or did she act in their favor because they showed her kindness and respect? Whatever it was, we can be certain that Joshua's men succeeded in convincing Rahab of the power and might of Yahweh, their God. Convincing her must have been easy because word had evidently spread throughout the land that Joshua and his army had been victorious in their conquests and that they were on their way to claim the land God had given their ancestors. Thus was Rahab prompted to say to them: "I know that Yahweh, your God, has given this land to you; we are frightened and the inhabitants of the land tremble before you" (2:9).

Before helping the spies escape, however, she tried to strike a deal with them: she made them promise that they would spare her entire family when they came back to conquer the city. Her request was that they return her kindness with kindness:

"Now then, swear to me by the LORD that, since I am showing kindness to you, you in turn will show kindness to my family; and give me an unmistakable token that you are to spare my father and mother, brothers and sisters, and all their kin, and save us from death" (2:12, NAB).

Rahab's background as a Canaanite and a prostitute probably honed her in the art of "wheeling and dealing," an art found among traders and those who have to learn to sell themselves in order to survive. According to Scripture scholars, the word Canaanite means "trader" in Semitic, and it captures in a name how other ancient people saw them.[8] No wonder the relatively poor tribes of Israel were struck by the wealth they saw among the Canaanites! But along with the glittering and prosperous material achievements came religious beliefs that clashed almost totally with Israel's stark faith in one God who is ruler, patriarch, and warrior, as well as protective mother, all in one.[9] In striking a deal with the spies, Rahab managed to get an oath from them.

At that time, oath-taking or oath-making was a common way of guaranteeing the fulfillment of a promise. Here God is usually invoked as guarantor of the oath, with the expectation that a broken or false oath would be punished.

What was the life of a harlot really worth that these two men would pledge their life to hers? As a woman whose character was of no consequence not only to spies on a secret mission but to society in general, Rahab was able to get the pledge of Joshua's men for as long as she would keep her end of the deal by not betraying their errand (2:14). To be given such a trust and oath must have built up her self-concept and self-respect as a person. Perhaps for the first time in her life she experienced what it is like to be a person, since she had been used to being treated as an object to be used, abused, and misused. Perhaps, too, for the first time in her life she was involved in a nobler mission—to save the life of her family and kinsfolk from total destruction. In order to give life and extend the life of others, she was willing to take grave risks. She had more to gain than to lose.

Anyway, as the story continues, her new-found hope and dignity seem to be giving her the energy and creativity to find ways to help the spies get out of the city. She gives them the following instructions: "Go up into the hill country . . . that your pursuers may not find you. Hide there for three days, until they return; then you may proceed on your way" (2:16, NAB). Grateful for everything that she is doing for them, the spies give her last minute instructions on how they will fulfill the oath she made them take—by tying a scarlet cord in the window through which she is letting them down. The cord is to be a mark to tell Joshua and his men not to destroy her house and to spare her house and those in it from death (vv. 15-21).

Concluding Scene—The Fall of Jericho: Joshua 6:20-25

As Joshua's army storms the city, they destroy everything in sight and put to the sword all living creatures in the city: men and women, young and old, as well as oxen, sheep and asses (6:20-21). This act of violence is not surprising because as mentioned earlier, Israel's literature[10] urges the eradication of the

Canaanite religion together with the Canaanite people. But as a fulfillment of the oath the two spies gave Rahab, they spare her, her family, and kinsfolk. She and her family then join the Israelite community (Josh. 6:17, 25).

According to Scripture scholars, the reference to Rahab in this scene is probably an addition to help connect the story of the fall of Jericho to the story of Rahab in chapter 2. These verses conclude the etiology begun in chapter 2 that explains the presence of Rahab and her family in the midst of Israel.[11] Nothing more is mentioned about her in the Book of Joshua. However, tradition believes that her entire family was received into Israel, apparently by marriage. One Jewish tradition makes her the wife of Joshua. Another tradition has it that she became the wife of Salmon, who could have been one of the spies who appealed to her for aid.[12] The Gospel of Matthew seems to confirm this tradition that Rahab married Salmon of the tribe of Judah and thus became the great-great-grandmother of David, through whose line is traced the Christ (Matt. 1:5; Ruth 4:18-22).[13]

Whatever tradition we might prefer to follow, the fact is that Rahab's marriage into Israel's faith and way of life saved her and elevated her status from a disdainful life of harlotry to one of dignity and grace as mother and as a woman of great faith. For staunch feminists, Rahab's liberation from the oppressive structure of a patriarchal and androcentric society may not be complete because she had to fit herself into the traditional and expected roles of women at that time, which were those of wife and mother. In these roles she was valued primarily as the bearer of sons or as a dutiful and hard-working wife. But for a harlot who was raised from a wretched condition of poverty and immorality, it was nonetheless an experience of liberating grace.

IMAGES OF FAITH AND SPIRITUALITY

In our re-reading of Rahab's story, we saw that the Deuter-onomic authors portrayed her, in her act of assisting Joshua's spies, as one motivated by a genuine fear of God and a belief that the God of Israel would conquer the city. In this portrayal the authors place on the lips of Rahab a profession of faith in Yahweh, the living God, who will entrust the country to the Israelites. Because of this faith Rahab will be saved, her name remembered and her good deeds praised by future generations. Let us look at her faith more closely and get a glimpse of the images of faith and spirituality that she is presenting to us.

In the Old Testament, "fear of God" is an important dimension of faith. Yet it does not necessarily mean that the basic principles of the law of love, as emphasized in the New Testament, are not also present. "In both Old Testament and New Testament there is a real though diverse blending of fear and love."[14] This religious "fear" that pertains to biblical revelation differs from the natural human fright experienced by every human being in the face of calamities of nature or attacks of enemy.[15] When one experiences imposing, extraordinary, or terrifying phenomena, one spontaneously senses a superior presence that makes one feel one's insignificance and nothingness. This is an ambiguous sentiment or feeling whereby the sacred is revealed under the aspect of the *tremendum* without further and more exact precision.[16] The Old Testament balances this sentiment with a genuine knowledge of the living God who shows divine power and greatness through many events, such as the victory of a small army against a mighty army or unusual happenings in the created universe like God's appearance to Moses by means of a burning bush (Exod. 3:6). This description of religious fear seems to fit Rahab's profession of faith, which contains a mixture of a real dread of the possibility of death and destruction from Joshua's advancing army and a genuine knowledge of the living God when she says:

> . . . I know that Yahweh, your God, has given this land to you; we are frightened and the inhabitants of the land tremble before you. We know how Yahweh dried up the waters of the Red Sea to let you cross when you came out of Egypt. We know what you did to the two kings of the Amorites who lived at the other side of the Jordan, to Sihon and Og, whom you destroyed by anathema.
>
> The news has frightened us, and everyone has lost cour-

age because of you, for Yahweh, your God, is God in heaven above as he is on earth below (2:9-11).

Rahab's profession reflects a true life of faith, where fear is held in balance by an opposite feeling of trust or confidence in the living God's mercy, justice, and love. Though she did not yet have a very personal relationship with the God of Israel, she believed in God's power and might and trusted the Israelite spies' word to fulfill their oath in God's name. So it is that faith in the living God, the source of assurance and hope, that completely banishes purely human fear.[17]

On the whole, the fear of God can be understood in so wide and profound a sense that it is simply identified with religion itself.[18] This is so because it leads one to grow in confidence and hope in God, to turn from one's evil ways and to respond in awe, reverence, and adoration before the living God.[19] Like the psalmist and Mary, Jesus' mother, we, too, together with Rahab and all those who have experienced God's saving power, can echo our praises to the living God as we say: Your mercy, God, extends from age to age to those who fear you! (Ps. 103:17; Luke 1:50).

Genuine "fear of Yahweh" leads not only to wisdom and knowledge of God (Prov. 2:5), but also to trust and confidence in God's deliverance. Rahab had obviously heard of God's mighty acts in delivering the Israelites from their bondage in Egypt when in her own words she said: "We know how Yahweh dried up the waters of the Red Sea to let you cross when you came out of Egypt" (2:10). Perhaps this was the kind of deliverance she was longing for—that she and her family might be rescued from the physical, psychological, and spiritual bondage into which their life of poverty had led them. Perhaps for Rahab the possibility of finally being delivered from bondage would be an exciting moment. Many of the poor in their simple faith continue to harbor the same kind of longing. In their hearts, they dream that someday God will lift them up from their poverty and misery.

Another dimension of spirituality that Rahab demonstrates to us is that of a faith that leads to true conversion of heart. Rahab—as a disdained prostitute—is not as much of consequence to us as what she became. Through her story, the biblical authors are repeatedly showing us that the "Bible deals with human beings in search of God."[20] God allows Oneself to be found through various ways. In Rahab's case, she found the living God through the experience of divine love and acceptance as mediated through ordinary human beings. This was when Joshua's spies valued her life by guaranteeing her safety and that of her family through an oath and when she and her entire family were accepted into Israel's faith through marriage. This experience of God gave her a chance to live life anew by departing from her former way of life to become a woman of great faith.

Luke later picks up the theme of Rahab's life story to demonstrate the forgiving and transforming power of Jesus' divine love in his story about the penitent woman who was known as a "public sinner," a prostitute (Luke 7:36-49). Her experience of God's mercy and forgiveness through Jesus' acceptance of her as a person restored her human dignity and gave her the grace and courage to change and transform her life. True faith focuses only on the quality of love and trust, and usually we love to the degree that we become aware of how much God has forgiven us.[21]

A faith that leads to conversion of heart also involves action or good works. Rahab's faith prompted her to act in favor of God's people. The women who were judged or labelled as "public sinners" in the New Testament (the penitent woman, the Samaritan woman, and the adulteress) did not only change their ways, some of them also put their faith in Jesus into action, such as the Samaritan woman who proclaimed the Good News to her own people. James, speaking of how character can be transformed, says, "Rahab the harlot will illustrate the point. Was she not justified by her works when she harbored the messengers and sent them out by a different route? Be assured, then, that faith without works is as dead as a body without breath" (James 2:25-26). Here, faith and action are two sides of the same coin. Our action has to be animated by our commitment to God in faith, while our faith is proven to be more authentic when it involves action.

TODAY'S RAHAB

Rahab's story ends on a happy note. But many of today's Rahabs are still awaiting liberation from the shackles of their oppression. To truly comprehend the situation of women, we have to penetrate the economic, cultural, and social structures in which their lives revolve. These are the structures that imprison many of them in situations similar to Rahab's before her conversion to Israel's faith. If liberation from oppression has to happen, it should begin in these structures.

Many developing and newly industrialized countries in Asia are reporting an increasing incidence of sexual crimes in their cities. It seems evident that as a city's tourist industry flourishes, so do prostitution, pornography, and related immoralities. Here are some scenes of prostitution in Asia.

One report[22] begins with these words: "Women? Oppress them! Destroy them and kill them!" to emphasize the activities going on since tourism became commercialized in Thailand. The report then proceeds to identify three groups of oppressors, destroyers, and killers: male foreigners, male nationals, and uneducated and ignorant parents of Thai girls.

The author describes how these three groups promote and perpetrate the sexual industry:

> ... For example, there are two books which have been written by men from other nations. *Bangkok by Night* by Lee Daniel is a guide for men who want to come to Bangkok only for one thing: SEX. ... The meat of his text is the part which explains why over 70% of all foreign visitors to Bangkok are unaccompanied males. Worse than this book is the book *Bangkok's Backstreets* by Bob Todd. It is not only a guide for the men to enjoy sex and the prostitutes but he looks down on all the women in Thailand ... His conclusion is all Thai women want to have sexual relations with the Westerners because it is an easy way to ... get into high society. ... There is also a video with the title *Foreign Body* by Tim Cooper, a documentary on sex tour-

ism in Thailand which shows all kinds of prostitution and inhuman sexual practices.

These men earn their living by promoting prostitution, by demeaning Thai women, and by breaking up families. The report continues:

> The second criminal example is men from inside the country. These are men who want to be rich without doing much work ... by using the bodies of the prostitutes to earn money. They look at the women as their prey. They go to the rural areas to look for girls who are innocent and ignorant. The girls are enticed to marry them or to get jobs in Bangkok. When the girls get to Bangkok they are forced to be prostitutes ... As Hosea 4:8 said, "They feed on the sin of the people, they are greedy for their iniquity."

Finally the report describes the third kind of criminal group: the uneducated and ignorant parents of Thai girls who practically sell their daughters because they also want to be rich. Although Thailand is not really a poor country, the level of education is low, especially in the rural areas. Uneducated farmers in the rural areas want modern conveniences and the comforts that are expected in a country undergoing rapid social change and development. The fastest way to obtain these things is to send their daughters to Bangkok to earn money. All that these parents know is that their daughters work, but they do not know how and what kind of work the girls do. Some parents even sell off their daughters in order to get money right away.

The report concludes that these three kinds of oppressors are responsible for forcing many women to become prostitutes and for giving Bangkok its reputation as one of the sex capitals of the world.

The experience of rising prostitution is not peculiar to Bangkok. It is in fact endemic in many of the world's cities. I suppose prostitution will be perpetrated and tolerated for as long as there are men who treat women and girls as objects for their own pleasure, for as long as there are poor and weak women who are ignorant of their dignity as human beings and allow themselves to be used, and for as long as there are oppressive and unjust societal structures. Prostitution is not only a sign but also a symptom of a much more serious social disease.

Another picture of today's Rahab is one that Columban priest Fr. Shay Cullen has painted for us through a video documentary he himself produced. (He works for a non-governmental agency that deals with victims of the sex industry.) The film shows the conditions of female prostitutes, including children, in Olongapo City in the Philippines.[23]

On the videotape, one woman being interviewed says that she has been a prostitute since she was fourteen. After twenty years in the trade, she reached a point where her body could no longer take the abuse. She was forced to sell her eleven-year-old daughter for 20 or 30 U.S. dollars, for how else would they survive?

Based on the interviews included in the film, many of the prostitutes hope and dream that someday American GIs will offer to marry them. To these women such a proposal would mean a real "break," similar to "striking a gold mine," their only chance to escape the miserable life of a prostitute. The film further shows Filipina brides-to-be of American servicemen being given special training and orientation in a "special school" designed for them within the U.S. military base. Their instructors are American women who teach them household roles and chores like budgeting and operating electronic household devices. The instructors also advise the Filipinas not to curtail their husbands' happiness but instead allow the men freedom to spend as much time as they want outside the home.

The whole presentation somehow gives the viewer the impression that these Filipina women are simply being groomed and trained to be submissive, domesticated creatures at the disposal of their American husbands. In many cases, the women are not even treated any differently from domestic helpers who in a sense are better off because at least they are paid for their services. Some of these new brides are expected to be slaves to their husbands. Whether or not the women are in fact treated well by their husbands is beside the point. Neither is it for us to judge the women's motives in seeking GI husbands as simply opportunistic or materialistic. The fact is, most of them who have been given the "break" are fortunate to have left their old way of life, which offered only misery, the risk of contracting serious diseases, and an uncertain future. Like Rahab, these GI brides have been given an opportunity to be raised from their wretched life of prostitution. To have such a new lease on life is for them a real blessing from God, an answer to their prayer for deliverance.

Today houses of prostitution are no longer like those Rahab kept. They have drastically changed with the entry of the Mafia, Yakuza, and other international crime syndicates in the scene. These places are no longer called "houses" but "sex farms" where poor, innocent, and ignorant women and girls are the prime victims. The business of trafficking of women is growing phenomenally in big cities and is fast becoming a big "multi-national establishment" with the support or connivance of corrupt government and military officials in third-world countries. For instance, according to recent reports, in Japan alone almost all of the Filipina women recruited as "entertainers" are forced to work as part-time prostitutes. Their handlers advertise them in magazines and billboards as being "for sale." These so-called entertainers are derogatorily called "japayukis," a term derived from prostitutes who used to accompany Japanese soldiers.[24]

Many of the women never imagined that they would end up in "sex farms" or as "japayukis."[25] This was the case of Liza Mamac,[26] a victim of trafficking of women. A city official named Nestorio Placer had convinced her to take a job as a hotel receptionist in Holland for a monthly salary of US $1,000. The supposed establishment was owned by the city official's millionaire-friend, a Mr. Schoeman. Liza took the offer in spite of her lack of qualification, thinking she could help alleviate her family's poverty. But the big opportunity turned out to be a "hell" she had to endure for several years. The "hotel" turned out to be a "sex farm" where several women, mostly from third-world countries, were being forced to work without pay as prostitutes. Liza tried to escape several times, but she would always get caught and consequently beaten. Her "liberation" came only after a couple of years, when the "sex farm" was raided by the police through information from a male customer who later became Liza's live-in partner.

After their rescue, Liza and another Filipina victim reported their case to the police authorities in Holland and filed rape and white slavery charges against Schoeman. Almost two years after her recruitment, the Dutch court sentenced the accused to two and a half years in prison. The accused was also ordered to pay Liza and her friend 1,500 guilders ($500) each. The amount of reparation was not even enough to buy Liza a one-way ticket back to the Philippines.

The fight was not over for Liza. When she returned to the Philippines with her live-in partner, she was determined to pin down Placer, Schoeman's Philippine counterpart in women trafficking. But because of the official's strong connections and influence in government, Liza and her women supporters found the effort an uphill battle. Nevertheless a local women's organization formally appealed to President Corazon C. Aquino not to reappoint Placer, citing Liza's documents, which were all sent to the office of the president. The request was granted and Placer was dropped from the judiciary.[27]

Liza's court case against Placer was not so lucky. After a five-year battle, the accused was acquitted. The court had based its decision on Liza's "questionable moral background and conduct." She was condemned for having lived previously with a married man. She was condemned for bravely testifying before the court as a pregnant and unmarried woman. Perhaps, if she had been a man, she would not have been disgraced for living with someone without marriage. However, her story, courage, and determination to seek justice touched many women who had heard of her undaunted response to her court defeat. When last heard about, she was set to file a *certiorari* through her legal counsel questioning the judgment of the court.

Although Liza has had setbacks in her court case, like Rahab she has experienced love and acceptance. The man who rescued her from the "sex farm" in Holland has become her steady companion and the father of her newborn daughter, Samantha. She may not have mentioned God in her personal testimonies, but through her partner's support and that of other concerned women in her area, she has experienced God's deliverance. This support has made her determined to continue her struggle for justice and to uphold the rights and dignity of poor and oppressed women.

PRAYING WITH RAHAB

Suggestions for Prayer and Reflection

• Read Rahab's story and that of today's Rahab. Do you see any connection? What are your feelings? Where are you in your attitudes toward those of ill repute in society? Are you among the passive or the self-righteous who from a distance would not care or would sit in judgment against the people who give their cities a bad reputation?

(Pause for reflection)

• *Prayer of Lament.* In silence, bring to your consciousness the many faces and images of today's Rahabs. Then read slowly the following lament:

> She spends her nights weeping,
> drenching her cheeks with tears.
> Who is there to comfort her
> among all her lovers?
> All her friends have betrayed her
> and have become her enemies.
> After her downfall
> [she] has gone into exile;
> but she finds no home in the nations
> where she sojourns;
> her pursuers have caught her up
> where there is no way out . . .
>
> She is at the mercy of her foes
> who enjoy prosperity and power.
>
> Greatly has [she] sinned;
> she has become a thing unclean.
> Honored before, but now despised
> by those who have seen her naked,

she herself groans in dismay
and turns her face away.

Her filth clings to her skirt,
she gave no thought to her doom,
and so her fall came suddenly,
with no one to offer comfort.
"Look, O Yahweh, upon my misery,
for my enemy has overcome me."
(Lam. 1:2-3,5a,8-9)

(Pause for reflection)

• *Prayer in Action.* Like the two spies of Joshua who gave their oath to spare Rahab and her family, be agents of hope and liberation to the despised, disdained, and rejected by society by:
- —joining women's organizations and groups dedicated to stopping the illegal recruitment and trafficking of women and children.
- —working against pornography and the use of sex and violence in media.
- —helping educate young, poor, and ignorant women about their rights, the country's situation, and what they can do to improve their lot without having to leave their country.

3

JEPHTHAH'S DAUGHTER

A Sacrificial Victim

In the Bible, daughters are not mentioned by name as often as are sons. This is not surprising. As we have already seen in the previous chapters, the Bible's androcentric bias and patriarchal context regard women and female offspring as inferior human beings. By not naming many of these women and daughters, the biblical narrators themselves reveal this bias. The nameless daughters must take their identity from their father. Compared to sons, daughters are of lesser value. As female offspring, they are not so highly prized. They are completely under the dominion of their fathers, who alone have the authority to decide for them. They do not have lives of their own, these being practically in their fathers' hands. Virgin daughters are as disposable as the concubine or the enslaved women captured in warfare.[1] Like pieces of property, sometimes fathers might sell their daughters as bondswomen, but not to foreigners (Exod. 21:7-8).[2] Once daughters marry, their fathers' authority over them is automatically passed on to their husbands.

It was not uncommon that some selfish and unthinking

55

fathers abused their rights over their daughters. For example, Lot offered his unnamed daughters to be raped by the violent mob in the city of Sodom (Gen. 19:8). Such aberrations did happen even if society may not have condoned them.

The story of Jephthah's daughter gives us a glimpse of the life situation of a female offspring in biblical times, especially during the time of the Judges. It comes to us through the Book of Judges, a collection of stories about several heroes from Israel's past.[3] This is the period between Joshua's death and before the monarchy. Her story appears within the context of her father's story, which proceeds as follows: a prologue (Judg. 10:6-16); the crisis of the time that necessitates Jephthah's recall from exile (Judg. 10:17-11:11); his negotiations with the Ammonites, Israel's enemy (Judg. 11:12-28); his vow and consequent victory (Judg. 11:29-40); and the defeat of the Ephraimites (Judg. 12:1-7). However, since our focus is on Jephthah's unnamed daughter, we shall look at her life more closely and re-read her story within the greater context of her father's life story.

But first, let us look at the recurring Old Testament theme that is the general context of the Book of Judges. Here God continues to be faithful and merciful to the people and to the judge, "but points out that the people forgot quickly the lesson and turned back to their evil ways, following after other gods and sinning worse than earlier generations had done."[4] Because of Israel's unfaithfulness, they are prone to the attacks of their enemies. During the time of the Judges, Israel still lived in tribal societies and lacked a centralized government. Israel thus was subject to threats of anarchy and extinction. When Jephthah appears on the scene, Israel is being threatened by the Ammonites.

In the midst of this threat, Jephthah the Gileadite emerges as Israel's "savior." Yet his coming into this role as Israel's judge has come as a paradoxical twist in his fate, a "marriage by convenience" arrangement. Earlier in his life, his own brothers and clan rejected him because he was an illegitimate son and his mother was a prostitute. Forced into exile, he ended up in the company of brigands and lived a Robin Hood-like existence as head of an outlaw gang.[5] But because the Gileadites need someone to fight for them against the threat of the Ammonites, they recall Jephthah to be commander of their army and eventually also their administrator.

Jepthath's first move as head of the army is to negotiate with the enemy who want their former land back. He uses as his argument a nation's right to keep that which God gives it in war. (Israel took possession of Canaan during the time of Joshua.) Having failed in his negotiations, Jephthath makes a vow to God. This is the point in which his daughter's story will be woven into his. Let us first read this account the way it is written in the Bible.

THE STORY OF JEPHTHAH'S DAUGHTER IN THE BIBLE

A Story within a Story: Judges 11:29-40

[29] The Spirit of Yahweh came upon Jephthah. He went through Gilead and Manasseh, passed through Mizpah of Gilead, and then entered the territory of the Ammonites.

[30] Jephthah made a vow to Yahweh: "If you make me victorious, [31] I shall sacrifice to you whoever first comes out of my house to meet me when I return from battle. He shall be for Yahweh and I shall offer him up through the fire."

[32] Jephthah crossed the territory of the Ammonites to fight against them and Yahweh gave him victory. [33] He pursued them from the city of Aroer to the entrance of Minnith and Abel Keramim, seizing twenty towns. So he defeated the Ammonites.

[34] When Jephthah returned home to Mizpah, his daughter came out to meet him. She was so happy to see her father that she danced to the sound of her tambourine. She was an only child; besides her he had no other daughter or son.

[35] When Jephthah saw her, he tore his clothes and cried out, "My daughter, you have shattered me; you have brought me misfortune. For I have made a foolish vow to Yahweh, and now I cannot take it back." [36] She answered

him, "Father, even if you have made such a foolish vow, you have to do to me just as you promised, for Yahweh has avenged you and crushed your enemies. [37] I only beg of you to give me two months to live with my companions in the mountains. There I shall lament because I will never marry." [38] Jephthah said to her, "Go then." And he sent her away for two months. She and her companions went to the mountains and wept because she would never marry.

[39] At the end of two months, she returned to her father and he fulfilled the vow he had made. The young girl had never known a man. From this comes the Israelite custom [40] that the daughters of Israel go out for four days annually to lament the daughter of Jephthah the Gileadite.

A RE-READING OF HER STORY

Our attention is first focused on Jephthah's vow. The episode begins with a biblical formula, "The Spirit of the Lord is upon Jephthah" (11:29), which clearly establishes divine permission for the events that will develop and predicts their successful outcome.[6] But Jephthah himself does not seem to show confidence in the presence of God's Spirit. Perhaps because of his lack of religious upbringing and the immorality that shrouds his background, he does not possess the kind of faith in God that should give him the conviction and the courage to act resolutely. Fraught with self-doubt about his capability to win the battle, he falls back to his "irreligious" upbringing. Unreflectively he resorts to making a "pagan" vow (11:30) for the source of his assurance in battle.[7] Right from the beginning, we see the incongruity of his action: making a vow to offer human sacrifice as a holocaust (a pagan practice) to the God of Israel who, according to Israel's faith, condemns such a sacrifice.[8] Clearly Jephthah does not know that what God wants most is faith and trust more than burnt offering or a holocaust of bulls or rams — and definitely not burnt offering of human flesh. Thus through the vow Jephthah is showing his unfaithfulness instead of showing true faith in the God who gave the territory to his ancestors. No wonder God initially responds to his vow in silence. But once victory is gained, God seems to accept the sacrifice, as evidenced by Jephthah's continuing military success. However, this simply suggests that the story must have originated in circles where human sacrifice was accepted.[9]

To put Jephthah's action in perspective, let us look at the pervading practices in those times among the ancient people. Making vows was a common practice, usually in times of major crisis, such as threat of war or serious illness. For instance, when the Canaanite king of Arad attacked Israel and took some prisoners, Israel made this vow to Yahweh: "If you put these people into my hand, I will consecrate their towns by anathema" (Num. 21:2). Then Yahweh responded and delivered the Canaanites into their hands, and their towns were destroyed (Num. 21:3). Vows ordinarily consisted of a promise to offer a sacrifice on condition that the deity would grant their request. The influence of pagan practices was still strong for people to believe that they had to make vows to appease God and to win divine favor.

Jephthah's vow contains both promise and condition. He begins with a condition ("If you make me victorious" — 11:30b), then offers a promise ("I shall sacrifice to you whoever first comes out of my house to meet me when I return from battle. He shall be for Yahweh and I shall offer him up through the fire" — 11:31). Because he lacks self-confidence and courage, he is forcing God's hand to make him successful, thus restraining God's Spirit to freely give it to him. Commenting on the movement of this vow, Trible writes:

> In moving from condition to outcome, Jephthah switches from direct address to a third-person reference for the deity: "Whatsoever comes forth ... shall belong to Yahweh."[10]

However, unlike his earlier bargaining and negotiations with the King of the Ammonites, this vow implicates the Lord in the outcome of the condition, for the sacrifice will be made to Yahweh.[11] Compared to the vow Israel made to Yahweh when the Canaanite king of Arad attacked Israel, Jephthah's vow implicates the destruction not only of the enemy but also of his own home and family. Israel's earlier vow only implicated the destruction of the enemy and their territories.

As expected, Jephthah wins the battle. To emphasize the greatness of his victory, we are treated to a litany of cities he trampled in his pursuit of Israel's aggressors (11:32-33). Successful, he goes home to Mizpah feeling the sweetness of success. What he wanted he has gotten. Now he is clearly in control, and his reputation as warrior and leader can no longer be disputed by his own people. But the consequence of this victory on his personal life and especially on his daughter would be tragic. Thus as we read the introductory line, "When Jephthah returned home to Mizpah," we are already filled with anxious anticipation as we are reminded of his own vow.

Who should be the first to come out of his house to meet him in victory? His only daughter. In fact, his only child. The text does not mention anyone else in his immediate family. His daughter's mother remains unnamed and unmentioned, as if to emphasize that his daughter is the only one of value Jephthah "possesses" in life. We are given an inkling of the impending consequencé of his vow and the high cost that his victory will exact from him (11:34). With his daughter's entrance into the scene, we come to know who shall be sacrificed and who shall bear the tragedy of his unfaithfulness.[12] Our hearts sink with Jephthah as we see the happy, innocent greeting of an only child who is proud of her father. She greets him joyfully with music and dancing, totally unaware of the misfortune about to befall her. While the whole of Gilead echoes the triumph of Jephthah, all the glory dies out as he sees his only daughter. His joy turns to sorrow, his gain to loss as he rends his clothes in anguish (11:35a). Only a cry of agony departs from his lips, followed by words of accusation directed at his daughter, "Alas, my daughter! you have brought me very low, and you have become the cause of great trouble to me; for I have opened my mouth to the LORD, and I cannot take back my vow" (11:35b, RSV). Notice that he immediately puts the blame for his misfortune on his daughter, not on himself. He is only thinking of himself, his own misfortune, his own feeling. He seems only to mourn for himself and not for his daughter. He does not seem to consider for a moment that it is his daughter, not he, who has to pay for his unfaithfulness and indiscretion. If anyone should be accused, it should be he! If anyone should speak words of accusation, it should be his daughter! But everything is reversed to demonstrate the powerless position of any woman or daughter in an abused patriarchy.

Is it his daughter's fault if she should joyfully rush out of the house to be the first to greet her own father as he returns triumphant in war? Is it her fault if she wants to be the first to celebrate her father's return with dancing and the sound of tambourines, as all women traditionally do when their army returns victorious from war?[13] Yet, all that was in Jephthah's mind was himself. Full of pride and selfishness, he has to rigidly fulfill the vow he has made, even if God and the Gileadites themselves never required him to make it to begin with. In our pondering, we can't help but think of his background and the kind of person he has become. It seems as if the judgment of generations past is upon him and his daughter. Commenting on this cycle of sin, Trible writes:

> If Jephthah suffered for the sins of his parents, how much more shall this child bear because of the machinations of her father. Unfaithfulness reaches into the third generation to bring forth a despicable fruit. "Is there no balm in Gilead?" (Jer. 8:22).[14]

Is there any way out for him from this meaningless vow? Is there any way by which his daughter can be spared from her impending doom? As an Israelite father, he has authority over his daughter. Life and death are in his hands. Yet sacrifice, even if unwarranted, seems to be only secondary to the irrevocability of his vow.

What a difference this story leaves us compared to Abraham's sacrifice of Isaac, his only son! Abraham's was a test of his faithfulness to Yahweh, while Jephthah's sacrifice of his only daughter is a stark demonstration of his unfaithfulness and misguided conscience. The sad thing about it is that he is not even conscious of his own defiance against Israel's faithful God. Thus, as a fruit of his unfaithfulness, his family lineage will be ended abruptly with his only child's death. "Faithfulness to an unfaithful vow has condemned its victim; father and daughter are split apart in deed and destiny."[15] And to think he could have done something about it!

Though Jephthah does not tell his daughter the specific content of his vow, the inevitability of his anguished words is sufficient. Both father and daughter know the tradition of offering a holocaust at that time — the entire victim (usually a bull, lamb, kid, or bird) is burnt to signify that the gift is total and irrevocable.[16] Yet she responds without resentment, rancor, anger, or self-pity.[17] Instead, with great familiarity in her words, using the possessive pronoun "my" in addressing her father, she responds:

> My father, if you have opened your mouth to the LORD, do to me according to what has gone forth from your mouth, now that the LORD has avenged you on your enemies, on the Ammonites (11:36, RSV).

The phrase "do to me according to what has gone forth from your mouth" is a biblical formula conveying the obedience of the speaker. It reminds us of Mary's response to the angel in Luke's gospel at the annunciation, "Let it be done to me as you have said" (Luke 1:38), but the circumstances and context are entirely different. Thus the implications of each response are also different. Here, Jephthah's daughter responds in humble obedience to death, the fruit of her father's unfaithfulness, while Mary responds to life, the fruit of her faithfulness and humble obedience to God's plan of salvation. Same words spoken centuries apart by two young women — one the unnamed daughter of a faithless father, the other a named daughter of faithful parents.

As if to lessen Jephthah's responsibility in fulfilling his vow, the narrator puts in his daughter's mouth the reason her father has to keep his word, "My father, if you have opened your mouth to the LORD, do to me according to what has gone forth from your mouth, now that the LORD has avenged you on your enemies, on the Ammonites" (11:36, RSV). Indeed the willingness of Jephthah's daughter to fulfill her father's vow is "comprehensible only if human sacrifice was a commonly accepted practice and that to be chosen as the sacrifice carried honor."[18]

Jephthah remains silent in the midst of his daughter's affliction. No words of comfort issue from his mouth. A huge abyss divides father and daughter. His feelings are all centered on himself. There is no room to feel for his daughter. The costly victory has driven them apart. She has to learn to take care of herself, for she can no longer rely on the care of her own father. He who has been her protector has become her accuser and executioner. She is totally alone and abandoned. Like a condemned criminal, she asks for a final request from her executioner, her own father:

> "Let this thing be done for me; let me alone for two months, that I may go and wander on the mountains, and bewail my virginity, I and my companions" (11:37, RSV).

Surely no father could deny such a simple request. She bargains for a little precious time, time to be alone with her friends and away from him. A time to lament with her friends not because she will die but because her life will end unfulfilled.[19] In biblical times, for a woman to remain a virgin and not to fulfill one's future role as wife and mother was considered a deprivation of God's blessing,[20] a curse, and a humiliation like sterility. Thus Jephthah's daughter needs to distance herself from her unfeeling and selfish father and to seek solace and understanding from her own companions, her fellow young women, as she bewails her virginity. For the first and last time, she shows independence, even if only temporary.

In just two words the father grants the request of his only daughter. "Go then!" Jephthah says to her. Those words would end the dialogue between father and daughter. Her words would be reserved for her friends in the solitude of the mountains, where she laments together with them the meaninglessness and unfulfillment of her young life and the finality of her leaving this world, without a trace that she has passed through it. After these last terse words of father to daughter, the only words available to us are those of the narrator, who tells us that true to her word, she returns to her father after two months so that he can fulfill his vow.

Yet the daughters of Israel would not want to bury her memory in oblivion. In solidarity with her, her faithful companions continued to mourn for her year after year until all the daughters of Israel would remember her from generation to generation:

> The daughters of Israel went year by year to lament the daughter of Jephthah the Gileadite four days in the year (11:40, RSV).

Though she remains unnamed, her story and her faithfulness to an unfaithful father are forever remembered in the pages of sacred history.

The narrator does not tell us that Jephthah mourned for his only daughter the way her friends and the daughters of Israel did. Neither does the narrator say that he remembered her and her self-giving. The narrator's silence on this gives us a sense that Jephthah seemed to have easily put aside his daughter's memory as he went on reaping successes for himself as a great military leader. Generations after his death, his name and his deeds continued to be remembered and acclaimed by Israel.

For the patriarchal authors of the Bible, Jephthah's military accomplishments seem far more significant than his daughter's supreme sacrifice in offering herself as her father's holocaust. He is remembered for his faith, while his faithlessness is seemingly forgotten. What a great paradox it is that centuries later the apostle Paul should count him among those who, through faith, "fought and conquered nations, established justice . . . valiant in battle, repulsed foreign invaders" (Heb. 11:32-33). Notice that there is no mention at all of how he sacrificed his only daughter for the sake of his military success.[21] We would like to believe that he did learn from his costly mistake and eventually learned to trust in the Spirit of God who made him triumph over Israel's enemies. We hope he did. We hope that at least a desire for atonement for his transgression was present when he finally offered his holocaust.[22] Though the narrator is silent[23] on this matter, there is a hope in us that the irrevocable and total gift of his daughter's life did purify his heart in the end.

But for us who have read and re-read the story of his daughter, her memory will forever linger in our consciousness. Like the daughters of Israel, we mourn for her and for all the women and daughters of the world who are sacrificial victims on the altar of human pride and selfishness. Though her life was fleetingly short, she becomes for us "an unmistakable symbol of all the courageous daughters of faithless fathers."[24]

IMAGES OF FAITH AND SPIRITUALITY

As we read the brief account of the life of Jephthah's daughter and examine the significance of her sacrifice and death, poignant images of faith linger in our minds, and movements of prayer are impressed upon us. Let us discuss some of these images and movements in light of what we have just read and re-read.

Like a lamb led to the slaughter or a sheep before the shearer [she] did not open [her] mouth (Isa. 53:7b).

These words of Isaiah echo in our hearts as we read and re-read the life of Jephthah's daughter. She responded to her father's faithlessness with faithfulness to the divine will, even if her image of God may have been limited or distorted. We cannot really fault her if she, like her father, imaged God as One who exacted the price of victory, for after all, in the Israelite culture and context, it is from one's father that one first learns who God is. What is of greater importance to us in this discussion are her innocence, purity of intention, and totality of obedience. We really cannot say that her obedience was blind because she perceived the meaning of her father's vow within the limited context of her knowledge of the Israelite faith and tradition. All her father said was, "For I have made a foolish vow to Yahweh, and now I cannot take it back" (11:35b). As a loving and obedient daughter, she placed herself completely at her father's disposal. She strongly believed that she was offering herself to the God of Israel. And so, obediently and humbly she submitted herself as a victim on her father's altar of sacrifice. As an obedient daughter, she offered her death in expiatory sacrifice and freely substituted herself for her sinful and faithless father. Her gift was total and irrevocable.

Although the writers in their patriarchal biblical bias never gave her sacrificial act any significance, we can do so from the perspective of the pattern of Christ's own self-offering as suffering servant and sacrificial lamb. Hers is a foreshadowing of Christ's sacrificial act. In Christ's offering we see God's response to our sins — God saving us through the suffering of the innocent and even more through the willing sacrifice of the One who takes the sin of the world upon himself. Christ's offering, in its bloody reality and its sacramental expression, sums up and fulfills the sacrificial economy of the Old Testament.[25] In Christ the Old Testament sacrifice is brought to perfection. In Christ the death of Jephthah's daughter is brought to fulfillment.

Generosity: Faith in Action

"Do to me according to what has gone forth from your mouth." These are not only words of obedience but words from a generous heart.

How do we really understand the word generosity? Based on its Latin root word, *gener*, meaning "to beget" or "to generate" (offspring), the act or process of begetting is essentially a choice for life. It involves self-giving.[26] The total submission of Jephthah's daughter to her father's vow can come only from a heart infused with generosity. We saw earlier that she never responded to her father with resentment, anger, or self-pity. Instead she surrendered herself to him — but not after bargaining for some time of solitude for herself. This is the paradox of her life: she remained a virgin, yet as a virgin she was able to give life, her very own. Yes, she lamented her virginity, for in the Old Testament mentality the goal of every woman was to become a wife and mother. Jephthah's daughter died without having had the opportunity to issue from her womb offspring that would continue the lineage of her family.[27] Her virginity was equivalent to sterility because she died deprived of the opportunity to give life, yet her very submission to such cruel and inhuman sacrifice was the ultimate act of giving life.

She was totally unselfish compared to the self-absorption and selfishness of her own father. Though nothing much is mentioned about her life of faith and prayer, her act of generosity is in itself a clear manifestation of the presence of an authentic and mature faith. Centuries later, another young woman named Mary generously and unselfishly said yes to what the angel announced to her. Her yes made God's plan of salvation possible. Jephthah's daughter made possible the salvation of one man, her own father. Through her submission to him in death, it is hoped that she allowed him to learn from his faithlessness and to grow in confidence in the Spirit of God that enabled him to win more wars without making another pagan vow to the God of Israel. What a costly sacrifice for the sake of one man! In contrast, Mary's yes to God's plan made possible the salvation of multitudes through the sacrifice of her Son.

Lamentation: A Prayer of Solitude and Solidarity

In the face of impending death, Jephthah's daughter felt her need for time — precious time to be in solitude and to lament with her friends. From her response to her father, we can glean two movements of prayer: a movement from loneliness to solitude and a movement from solitude to solidarity. But first let us re-read her response:

> "I only beg of you to give me two months to live with my companions in the mountains. There I shall lament because I will never marry" (11:37).

Another translation makes her request sound stronger: "Let me have this favor. Spare me for two months, that I may go off down the mountains to mourn my virginity with my companions" (11:37b, NAB). The Jerusalem Bible translation gives us yet another nuance to her request: "Let me be free for two months."

These three different translations give us a sense of the impact on her of her obedience to her father's vow. She suddenly realizes her need for time away from her father so she may sort out her feelings. Although her initial response to her father already seems to indicate the presence of total acceptance (11:36), from the human perspective she still needed time to let the reality of her yes sink in. The length of time — two months — does not seem to have any biblical significance as other numbers have. Perhaps it is to indicate that she was not ready emotionally and spiritually for the immediate execution of her father's vow.

We have seen that her father's vow drove a deep wedge between father and daughter. The father emotionally abandoned the daughter with his intention to carry out the vow, like cutting her off totally from the land of the living. A person in this condition would naturally feel lonely. Henri Nouwen has made an important distinction between loneliness and solitude.[28] Loneliness is the condition of one who feels abandoned, while solitude is the experience of a subtle, aching void that can only be filled by divine presence. Prayer that enables one to unite oneself with God can begin to fill this void and ease the aching. But full and final satisfaction is reserved until one has left this earthly pilgrimage and rests in God's bosom.[29]

In going to the mountains, Jephthah's daughter wanted to change her loneliness to solitude, to feel free ("Let me be free for two months") for the first and last time, and to experience the support of her friends. But why the mountains? What is so significant about them? She could have chosen to go somewhere else. Jephthah's daughter seems to be urgently motivated by religious reasons in choosing to go to the mountains. In biblical literature, there is something mystical about mountains. Abraham offered his son Isaac on a mountain in Moriah (Gen. 22). God appeared to Moses twice on a mountain—Mt. Horeb or Sinai—first in a burning bush, then later to give him the Commandments.

Jephthah's daughter went to the mountains to lament her virginity. When one laments, one prays to God so intensely that one spills out to God one's raw feelings, questions, and doubts, hoping to understand the incomprehensibility of one's suffering. Even if no divine answer comes, the very act of crying out to God in lamentation "re-establishes lines of communication in prayer and satisfies our human need to be heard, even if God seems to be silent."[30] The prayer of lament presupposes that the "pray-er" had experiences of intimacy with God in the past. For in this form of prayer, one freely speaks to God as if God were a friend or loved one.[31] The mountain seems to be the only place left for Jephthah's daughter to feel truly free to express herself. There she is able to move from loneliness to solitude.

How necessary it is to give ourselves time for prayer and solitude when we are confronted with an incomprehensible situation of great suffering. We need to distance ourselves, temporarily at least, from people who have hurt us deeply in order to allow our wounds to heal and to give ourselves the space to sort out our feelings. We need time and distance to enable ourselves to move from loneliness to solitude and from denial to acceptance.

It was also in the mountains that Jephthah's daughter felt true solidarity. Here she experienced kinship with the womenfolk, seemingly her only true companions in time of strife. They lamented with her, letting her feel that she was not alone in her suffering. In solidarity her friends did not allow her memory to die. Through them it was possible for her to live on in a different way, not through human progeny but through human memory. Through solidarity her memory is kept alive among the daughters of Israel. Through her story we are reminded that we can lighten one another's struggles, pains, and burdens through solidarity. And through solidarity, we can continue to remind the world that one person's sacrifice is not forgotten. What Jephthah could not do for his own daughter, the women did!

The prayer of lament becomes a true expression of solidarity. It is a crucial part of dealing with the present issues of oppression and injustice continually being experienced by women, daughters, and girls today. In the prayer of lament, grief and anger belong to our full response to the situation, for it helps us move toward solidarity.

TODAY'S DAUGHTER OF JEPHTHAH

The figure of Jephthah's daughter continues to haunt us today. We see her image in the many homeless and hopeless children and young girls loitering in city streets. We see her in the children and teenagers whose young lives are wasting away because of malnutrition or drug addiction. We see her in the young girls who are practically sold into white slavery or prostitution by greedy and ignorant parents. We see her in the young daughters who are sexually abused by their own fathers. We see her in the women factory workers who toil under hazardous and oppressed conditions and whose health and lives are sacrificed daily for the sake of corporate profit. We see her in the women of the squatter areas and urban centers whose lives and dreams remain unfulfilled for lack of opportunities. The figure of Jephthah's daughter, of her young and unfulfilled life, is everywhere and anywhere.

Now and then her image confronts us through the front pages of newspapers. A recent headline read: "Thirteen Women Workers Burned to Death." As the story went, the young women were trapped in the raging fire of a garment factory. Investigation simply confirmed what was common knowledge: the factory building was a fire hazard and had no fire escapes. It was only one of many factories that have been declared as unsafe and unfit for workers, yet the government closes its eyes to these places because the garment industry is the Philippines' second biggest dollar-earning nontraditional export. Not too long ago, the international news section of a national daily carried a similar story about several garment workers, mostly women, burned to death in Bangladesh.

The thirteen who were burned to death in Manila are only a few of the many sacrificial victims whose lives are offered daily on the altar of capitalism and in exchange for a third-world country's economic success.

For the sake of economic success, many women, daughters, and children have to be sacrificed daily in the Third World. A common scenario in these countries is for poverty-stricken parents to encourage their children to seek the pot of gold in distant shores, even if they have to get there through illegal recruiting agencies. For instance, in the Philippines, these agencies (some of them are mere fronts of the Yakuza crime gang) go to the provinces or to the urban poor areas to procure women to be sent to Japan as "entertainers." Sometimes they give two hundred pesos (less than US $10) to the parents of these young women as goodwill money. Others promise heaven and earth for their future. Greed and the desire for a life of comfort goad parents to practically "sell" their daughters to these agencies. Before being sent abroad, the girls are packed like sardines in "talent offices" in Manila or Cebu where they are supposed to be auditioned for three songs or three dances by the Philippine Overseas Employment Administration (POEA), a government agency, for certification as "professional" entertainers. "This is where corruption in the Philippine Overseas Employment Administration comes in because by all standards these 'entertainers' can neither sing nor dance in a professional manner."[32] These young women almost always end up in prostitution. Most are physically assaulted and brutalized by their Japanese "bosses" and customers and are often forced into drug addiction and virtual enslavement. Their dreams of a better life are shattered along with their battered bodies. Clearly, they are sacrificial victims of men's violence and lust and of parents' greed and ignorance.

Amnesty International paints another portrait of today's daughter of Jephthah. A national daily[33] carried a portion of the international organization's report entitled "Abuses Push Women into Front Line." According to Amnesty International's report:

> Women are experiencing violence under repressive governments. A pregnant detainee is punched in the stomach by police officers; an elderly woman is raped in front of her family by police officers; a young wife is killed because she refuses to stop searching for her "disappeared" husband; a woman is tortured to make her husband confess.

Another poignant image of Jephthah's daughter today is that of the street children. As one listens to their individual stories, one can't help but feel anger and consternation at the many fathers (and sometimes even mothers) who continually force their own children to beg as a means of supporting their drinking and gambling habits or simply for their own survival. It is a pathetic situation, a high price to pay for a country's economic "boom."

This was Aying's daily lot before she entered Dangpanan (literally, "shelter"), a home for street girls in Cebu City, Philippines. She and three younger siblings were constantly being subjected to battering by their own father whenever they could not bring in money from begging in the streets. Although still able-bodied, the father is a drunkard who long ago reneged on his responsibility to his family and turned to alcohol to escape the hardships of destitution. Whenever he had money in his pocket, he would abandon his family. He would return drunk and would either batter his wife and children or harass the latter to beg for more money from passersby. The wife has tuberculosis and has been depending on occasional charity for her medication. Home to this family is a pushcart. When the children are not begging, they are scavenging in the city's garbage dump hoping to find something to eat, perhaps some leftover food or something of value they can sell at the junk shop. One of the youngest siblings died of a congenital disease worsened by extreme poverty and malnutrition. They had to lay his body out on the sidewalk to collect enough money from sympathetic passersby for his burial. The parish priest at a nearby church and a religious sister helped the family bury the dead child. Aying and two other siblings were taken into the home for street girls. The two youngest daughters remain with their mother to help her beg for food. Like most street children, Aying and her siblings have already had their lives physically, psychologically, and morally damaged beyond repair. Not only has their father abandoned them, even society has given up on them.

Today's street children are like maggots that are multiplying fast in the city streets but people pretend not to see them. People would rather turn their faces away and blame the system for their existence, not realizing that we all are to blame for their suffering and unfulfilled lives. Street children are truly the sacrificial victims not only of their fathers' irresponsibility and selfishness but also of society's neglect and callousness. Who will lament for them? Will the daughters of our nation lament with them?

PRAYING WITH JEPHTHAH'S DAUGHTER

Suggestions for Prayer and Reflection

• Read and re-read her story. Do you see some connection between her story and that of today's women and children?

What stirred within you as you read the biblical and contemporary stories?

(Pause for reflection)

• *Prayer of Lament.* While imagining Jephthah's daughter and while thinking of the contemporary scenarios and situation, silently read either of the following prayers of lament:

(1) From the Lamentations of Jeremiah:

> Cry out to the Lord;
> > moan, O daughter Zion!
> Let your tears flow like a torrent
> > day and night;
> Let there be no respite for you,
> > no repose for your eyes.
>
> Rise up, shrill in the night,
> > at the beginning of every watch;
> Pour out your heart like water
> > in the presence of the Lord;
> Lift up your hands to him
> > for the lives of your little ones
> Who faint from hunger
> > at the corner of every street . . .
>
> Dead in the dust of the streets
> > lie young and old;
> My maidens . . .
> > have fallen by the sword;
> You have slain on the day of your wrath,
> > slaughtered without pity.
> > > > (Lam. 2:18-21)

(2) From a Contemporary Source:[34]

> How long, O Lord, how long
> must agony continue

violence be hidden
families lie
women and children live in fear?

How long, O Lord, how long
must women's silent screams fill the universe
and darkness invade their lives
because neighbors
    police
    and church
    close ears and eyes?

How long,
before Cain is banished
and people no longer hide behind
"Am I my sister's keeper?"

How long before women are
no longer isolated
    blamed
    burdened
    forced to accept crimes in home and family
    which on the street, against another person,
    would lead to public outcry
    "assault!" "battery!" "rape!"?

How long, O Lord
will women and children be treated as chattels
for the use of men?
Are the battered bodies of women
the sacrifice you claim
or have we turned from Christ to Moloch
unable to live by gentle love but only violent hate?

How long will battered women be the punching bags
    of men,
and their children grow up in fear?
How long will the church pretend that all its families
    are loving

all its men good fathers
all its teaching true and benign?

When will women be released from vicious marriages and
men forced to come to terms with the evil of their violence? When will divorce be seen as the burial of dead
relationships and the beginning of new life for abused people?

How long, O Lord,
will silence
ignorance
lies
enslave women
and make mockery of "love" and "family."
— Ann Wansbrough

• *Prayer of Solidarity.* Remain in silence and be attentive to
what stirs within you. Then lift up to God the lives of all the
daughters of Jephthah today.

• *Prayer in Action.* Show your solidarity with all the daughters,
women and girls who are sacrificial victims in our society today
by:
 — telling their story so others may become aware of their
   oppression and suffering and so they may not remain
   unnoticed and forgotten. The friends of Jephthah's daughter did not only lament with her; they repeated her story
   year after year to keep her memory alive.
 — volunteering some of your time for street children.
 — involving yourself with an organization that is working for
   women's concerns and structural change in society.

4

RUTH AND NAOMI

Companions through Life Transitions

In biblical times, the idea of an independent woman was totally unacceptable. In fact, it was unthinkable. Independence and womanhood were a contradiction in terms from the perspective of a highly patriarchal society. In the worldview of such a society, a woman was always seen as a dependent member of a family. She was dependent upon her father if unmarried, upon her husband if married, and upon her adult son if widowed. But of the three possible positions of women, widowhood was the most difficult because a widow could not inherit from her husband; she was merely a part of her eldest son's inheritance.[1] If she was childless, she returned to her father's house (Gen. 38:11; Lev. 22:13).[2] If she was both fatherless and childless, she would be doubly unfortunate because without a right to own property, she would be homeless. Besides, a woman who had no man to defend her rights was oftentimes highly vulnerable to the extortion of a creditor (2 Kings 4:1-37) and to any type of oppression.[3] She was also at the mercy of dishonest judges. A widow therefore was destined to a life of extreme poverty.

This is the implied situation when the Book of Ruth opens. The story's setting leaves us with three widows: Naomi, the mother-in-law; and her two widowed daughters-in-law, Ruth and Orpah. Before we explore the story itself, however, let us consider some general background information about this book which is named after one of the three widows, Ruth, the faithful daughter-in-law of Naomi.

The Book of Ruth is one of the immortal love stories in the Bible. It is set within history during the period of the judges[4] and takes as its characters and events ordinary people and mundane life situations. Its purpose is not only to entertain and delight its audience with plot complications, suspense, and a satisfying denouement but also to instruct and to hold up to its readers and listeners authentic models of covenantal faith.[5] In four brief chapters, the writer has created unforgettable characters and a plot that involves the reader from beginning to end. What the Mosaic Law spells out only in theory, the story's characters—Ruth, Boaz, and Naomi—actually live out in practice.[6]

Although the story ends happily like a fairy tale, the situation around which it develops its plot depicts the real-life problems, struggles, and oppressive situation of Israel's poor in general and the widows of biblical times in particular. Even today's reader can easily find parallelisms in the situation of poverty and oppression that persists in present-day society. Thus the story's closeness to life enables us to identify with its characters, to sympathize with their situation, and to rejoice at the solution of their problems.[7]

RUTH'S STORY IN THE BIBLE

Although the book itself consists of only four short chapters, it would be too lengthy to quote the entire book in this chapter. I will simply summarize each chapter, except for the second, which will be quoted in its entirety. Only passages that have a direct bearing on our discussion on prayer and spirituality and which will highlight the main characters' actions and responses will be quoted within the summary of each chapter.

Summary of First Chapter: Migration to Moab and Return to Bethlehem

During the time of the judges, Elimelech of Bethlehem, together with his wife Naomi and his two sons, Mahlon and Chilion, migrated to Moab to escape a famine in Judah. Elimelech died in Moab. His sons married two Moabite women, Orpah and Ruth. The two sons also died, however, leaving two childless widows with their widowed mother-in-law. Naomi decided to return to Bethlehem, the land of her birth. Her daughters-in-law went with her. While they were on the road, she urged her daughters-in-law to return to their mothers' houses, for she was unsure of what future they would have with her. Orpah sorrowfully returned to her family, but Ruth clung to her mother-in-law in spite of Naomi's prodding that she follow Orpah's decision. The following is Ruth's response to her mother-in-law:

[16] Ruth replied, "Don't ask me to leave you. For I will go where you go and stay where you stay. Your people will be my people and your God my God. [17] Where you die, there will I die and be buried. May Yahweh deal with me severely if anything except death separates us." [18] Realizing that Ruth was determined to go with her, Naomi stopped urging her.

[19] So the two went on till they reached Bethlehem. Their arrival set the town astir. Women asked, "Can this be Naomi?" [20] She said to them, "Don't call me Naomi. Call me Mara for Yahweh has made life bitter for me. [21] I came away full but go back empty. Why call me Naomi, when Yahweh has afflicted me?"

[22] Thus it was that Naomi returned from Moab with her Moabite daughter-in-law and arrived in Bethlehem as the barley harvest began (1:16-22).

Second Chapter: Ruth Gleans in the Field of Boaz

[1] Naomi had a well-to-do kinsman, Boaz, from the clan of her husband Elimelech. [2] And Ruth the Moabite said to

Naomi, "Let me go to pick up the left-over grain in the field whose owner will allow me that favor." Naomi said, "Go ahead, my daughter." ³ So she went to glean in the fields behind the harvesters. It happened that the field she entered belonged to Boaz of the clan of Elimelech.

⁴ When Boaz came from Bethlehem, he greeted the harvesters, "Yahweh be with you." They returned the greeting, "Yahweh bless you."

⁵ Noticing Ruth, Boaz asked the foreman of his harvesters, "To whom does that young woman belong?"

⁶ The foreman replied, "She is the Moabite who came back with Naomi from the country of Moab. ⁷ She came this morning and asked leave to glean behind the harvesters. Since then she has been working without a moment's rest."

⁸ Boaz said to Ruth, "Listen, my daughter. Don't go away from here to glean in anyone else's field. Stay here with my women servants. ⁹ See where the harvesters are and follow behind. I have ordered the men not to molest you. They have filled some jars with water. Go there and drink when you are thirsty." ¹⁰ Bowing down with her face to the ground, she exclaimed, "Why have I, a foreigner, found such favor in your eyes?"

¹¹ Boaz answered, "I have been told all about you — what you have done for your mother-in-law since your husband's death, how you have gone with her, leaving your own father and mother and homeland, to live with a people you knew nothing about before you came here. ¹² May Yahweh reward you for this! May you receive full recompense from Yahweh, the God of Israel, under whose wings you have come for refuge!"

¹³Ruth said, "May I prove worthy of your favor, my lord. You have consoled your servant with your kind words, though I am not the equal of your maidservants."

¹⁴ Boaz called her at mealtime, "Come over, have some bread and dip it in the wine." As she sat among the reapers, he handed her some roasted grain. She ate her fill and had some left over.

¹⁵ When she rose to glean, Boaz instructed his men, "Let

her glean even among the sheaves and do not scold her. [16] And pull some stalks from the bundles; leave them scattered for her to glean." [17] She worked until evening and when she threshed what she had gleaned it amounted to about an ephah. [18] Ruth carried back to town the threshed barley, which she showed to her mother-in-law. She also gave her what she had left over from lunch.

[19] Naomi asked her daughter-in-law, "Where did you glean today? Where did you work? May the man who took notice of you be blessed." Ruth told her mother-in-law about the owner of the field where she had worked. "His name is Boaz," she said. [20] Naomi exclaimed, "May Yahweh bless him! God indeed is merciful both to the living and the dead. This man is a close relative, one with a right of redemption over us."

[21] Ruth continued, "He even told me to stay with his servants until they finish harvesting the grain." [22] Naomi said, "It will be better for you, my daughter, to go out with his maidservants than to go working in some other field where harm might come to you."

[23] Ruth, therefore, stayed close to the maidservants of Boaz, gleaning until the end of the wheat and barley harvests. And she continued living with her mother-in-law.

Summary of the Third Chapter: Boaz Encounters Ruth

Naomi urged Ruth to seek marriage with Boaz since he was her kinsman, although remote. Ruth obeyed her mother-in-law's instructions (3:1-4) and crept under Boaz's mantle while he slept on the harvesting floor. At midnight he awoke and felt someone lying at his feet. Startled to find a woman, he asked for her identity. Here is Ruth's response and the rest of the scene as narrated to us in the Bible:

"I am Ruth, your servant. Spread the corner of your cloak over me for you are a kinsman who has right of redemption over me." [10] Boaz said, "May Yahweh bless you, my daughter! This kindness of yours now is even greater than that which you have shown earlier, for you have not gone after young men, rich or poor. [11] Have no fear, my daughter; I will do for you all that you ask, since all my townsmen know that you are a worthy woman. [12] It is true that I am a close relative, but there is another still closer. [13] Stay here for the night. In the morning, if he wants to claim you — good! But if not — as surely as Yahweh lives — I will claim you myself. Lie here till morning."

[14] She lay at his feet till morning and got up before anyone could be recognized. For Boaz said, "It must not be known that a woman came to the threshing floor." [15] Then turning to Ruth, Boaz said, "Hold out the mantle you are wearing." She did so and he poured into it six measures of barley. He helped her lift the bundle, then went back to town.

[16] Ruth returned home to her mother-in-law, who asked, "How did you fare, my daughter?" She told her everything [17] and added, "He gave me these six measures of barley because, as he said, he did not want me to go back to my mother-in-law empty-handed."

[18] Naomi said, "Wait, my daughter, till you learn what happens, for he will not rest until it is settled today."

Summary of the Fourth Chapter: The Resolution and Conclusion of the Story

After having accepted the implied proposal of marriage, Boaz first had to redeem Ruth from a nearer kinsman, according to the levirate law.[8] The kinsman forfeited his claim for fear of endangering his own estate. Boaz married Ruth, and their son was Obed, the grandfather of David.

A RE-READING OF THE STORY OF RUTH

First Chapter: Migration to Moab and Return to Bethlehem (1:1-22)

The opening verses of the first chapter reflect conditions typical of life in ancient Palestine. Families usually migrated because of the frequent occurrence of famine in the area. The country of Moab, with a narrow strip of well-watered and fertile land running north and south in its center, became a refuge for migrant families. This was why Elimelech, Naomi, and their two sons migrated there.

This kind of scenario is familiar even today. To escape economic difficulties caused by drought in the countryside or increased militarization in third-world rural areas, people flock to the cities and town centers seeking either the "pot of gold" or refuge from military oppression. There is continued migration of professionals from third-world to first-world countries in search of better opportunities. Affluent nations can offer better jobs, greater economic success, and a brighter future.

Thus migration for the sake of survival and a better life is an understandable occurrence in any generation and culture. Biblical literature records a number of such departures. We can recall Joseph and his family moving to Goshen (Gen. 47:27) or a widow following Elisha's advice and moving to the land of the Philistines (2 Kings 8). So Elimelech's decision to leave Bethlehem of Judah together with his family was understandable, even if going to Moab and settling among the people there was unexpected in light of the prohibition in Deuteronomy 23:4-5,7 which says:

> The Ammonite or Moabite shall never be admitted into the assembly of Yahweh even after the tenth generation, because when you came forth from Egypt, they did not go out to meet you with bread and water, but instead they hired Balaam . . . to curse you. You shall never share your prosperity or happiness with these peoples.[9]

However, based on historical facts, relations with Moab were sometimes hostile and sometimes friendly. The story implies that Elimelech's family migrated at a time when the atmosphere in Moab was more favorable for the Judean family to settle there. Perhaps the author also had a purpose in choosing such a setting. We shall see as the story progresses.

To alert us immediately to the development and historical probability of the story, the author also gives the characters names which in Hebrew have symbolic meanings. The husband and father *Elimelech* means "my God is king"; the wife and mother *Naomi* means "pleasant"; the two sons' names, *Mahlon* and *Chilion,* mean "sickness" and "wasting," respectively.[10] After the naming of the family members, the narrator tells us what happens after they have settled in Moab — death strikes the male members of Naomi's family. First, Elimelech dies. Naomi is left with her two sons, who later marry native women. But after ten years the sons also die without leaving any sons. Naomi, a widow of advanced age with no sons but only non-Jewish and childless daughters-in-law, is therefore destined for a life of destitution and social oppression.

In her emptiness and poverty, she decides to return to the land of her birth because the famine there is over. Perhaps she thinks her own townspeople will be kinder to her in her poverty than if she were to remain in Moab as a foreigner and widow. Her two widowed daughters-in-law initially go with her. But along the way, knowing that she cannot offer them any future, she urges them to return to their "mother's house." She just cannot impose her desire and longing for her own land and people on her already suffering daughters-in-law, nor can she deprive them of the small consolation that their own homeland would provide them. Besides, she knows that it would be much more difficult for them, being foreigners, to remarry in her homeland than in theirs because Hebrew laws discourage inter-marriage with foreigners.[11]

Here Naomi is projected as a practical person. She sees the time not for grieving but for doing something in a situation that needs some practical solution. Naomi's use of the unusual phrase "mother's house" is to be noted, for a house is usually designated as one's father's.[12] Some commentators believe it is used to symbolize or to emphasize the absence of men in the women's lives.[13] From another perspective it can also be seen as words of consolation to the suffering women, for the word "mother" evokes images of love, care, and nurturance — experiences one would long for in a time of brokenness.

From the very beginning the author makes us feel the pattern of emptiness in the life of Naomi to prepare us for the ensuing events. Biblical scholar Pauline Viviano comments on this motif:

The emptiness of the land (famine) causes Naomi to leave the land. The emptiness of the land gives way to the emptiness of Naomi in the loss first of husband and then sons. Naomi dismisses her daughters-in-law because her "emptiness" cannot be cured. She is too old to give birth again. Naomi's emptiness is accentuated when she contrasts her previous abundance with her present destitution (1, 21).[14]

Orpah heeds Naomi's advice and returns to her people, but Ruth refuses. Although the motif of emptiness is strongly accentuated here, we see that Naomi is not totally empty, for Ruth, in her decision to cling to her, would not allow her mother-in-law to return to her homeland totally empty and alone. Ruth vows to accompany Naomi through a perilous journey into an uncertain future. Ruth responds to her mother-in-law's prodding to leave her with words of loyalty and devotion:

'Do not press me to leave you and, to turn back from your company, for

'wherever you go, I will go,
wherever you live, I will live.
Your people shall be my people,
and your God, my God.
Wherever you die, I will die
and there I will be buried.
May Yahweh do this thing to me
and more also,
if even death should come between us!' (1:16-17, JB).

Ruth pledges covenant fidelity and claims as her own Naomi's location, people, and God.[15] In her beautiful and moving response, Ruth clings not to a past but to a present — not to a male through whom she may achieve power and access but to a female, one who needs her, one for whom she will provide protection, care, and access.[16] Ruth thus gives to her mother-in-law the only thing she possesses — her very self! Even if society destines both of them for a life of extreme poverty as widows, they still have each other. We can still see this kind of attitude among simple poor families. They are extremely loyal to their own members and would sacrifice for and protect one another in good times and in bad.

Together the two widows now turn their faces resolutely toward Palestine and the city of Bethlehem (1:19a). The distance between Moab and Bethlehem is only about 120 miles, but this stretch represents a long, fatiguing, and dangerous trek in this period, especially for two women who have neither money beyond their barest needs nor protector.[17] It is this journey through barren places that will perhaps bring them closer to each other and causes them to cling more closely together for protection, comfort, and support.

As they reach Bethlehem, the town is astir, prompting the women to notice Naomi's changed appearance after a long time since her departure for Moab (1:19b). Perhaps, too, her bearing has changed, prompting the women to comment on her name, which no longer seems to carry her identity (Naomi means "pleasant"). Gone is the pleasantness in her appearance and bearing. Naomi responds by naming her changed situation with a change of name. She says to them: "Don't call me Naomi. Call me Mara for Yahweh has made life bitter for me. I came away full but go back empty. Why call me Naomi, when Yahweh has afflicted me?" (1:20-21). Because of her emptiness she testifies that the name Naomi no longer fits her, for God has afflicted her. This, we find, is a recurring theme in the Old Testament: a woman's fatherless, husbandless, and sonless state is believed to be a sign of God's curse. The problem Naomi poses here is the eternal question asked by any sufferer: Why would God allow this tragedy to happen to me? It is presumed that God is in control, but when the control seems unreasonable, God gets the blame.[18] Naomi accepts her situation with resignation, believing that God has caused this misery in her life. But still unknown to both widows, Bethlehem, which means "house of bread," will be kinder to them. The city whose famine forced Elimelech and his family to migrate to Moab now welcomes them at harvest time.

Second Chapter: Ruth Gleans in the Field of Boaz (2:1-23)

The chapter has two episodes consisting of two interactions: one between Boaz and Ruth and the other between Ruth and

Naomi. It begins with the narrator giving us information that will set the stage for the next scene. It states that Boaz is a "covenant-brother" of Elimelech, therefore a kin which in the levirate law would open a marital possibility for Ruth.[19]

The narrator immediately makes Ruth initiate the next act by asking Naomi for permission to glean grain in the fields of some landowner who might be kind enough to let her do so. This projects Ruth as knowledgeable about Israel's law regarding care for the poor in spite of her being a foreigner. The law specifies concern for the poor, for widows, foreigners, and orphans, and provides for their care in certain ways, such as allowing them to glean the fields. The poor, the widows, and the orphans can gather the grain that the threshers dropped or passed over and keep what they collected. The landowner, on the other hand, is not allowed to glean his fields after harvesting a crop, for what remains in the field is supposed to be left for the poor (Lev. 19:9-10, 23:22, Deut. 24:19).[20]

With Naomi's consent, Ruth begins her role as provider for both of them (2:2). By a fortunate coincidence she gleans in Boaz's fields although the fact that he is a relative of Elimelech is yet unknown to Ruth (2:3). Boaz arrives in the field and greets his harvesters with a blessing, indicating the covenant environment in which they live (2:4). From his vast ownership, we can also conclude that Boaz is a man of considerable means. He notices Ruth and asks the servant in charge about her: "To whom does this young woman belong?" (2:5). In a patriarchal society, as we have already seen, the woman is part of a man's possession and does not have an identity apart from the man. The servant in charge replies in accordance with Boaz's question, not naming Ruth but defining her by her place of origin and her family connection with Israel and then adding a favorable comment about her industriousness (2:6-7).[21]

We can now gather from Boaz's kind treatment of Ruth that he feels a certain responsibility for her, knowing that she is related to his dead relative, although he makes no allusion to being a relative. This is indicated in the following verses by the way he addresses her using a relational or diminutive word, "daughter," and by his instructions to her:

"Listen, my daughter. Don't go away from here to glean in anyone else's field. Stay here with my women servants. See where the harvesters are and follow behind. I have ordered the men not to molest you. They have filled some jars with water. Go there and drink when you are thirsty" (2:8-9).

She responds to Boaz as a servant would to her master after being shown some favor. In a submissive and reverential stance (falling on her face and bowing to the ground), she expresses wonder and surprise that she, a poor foreigner, should be shown such favor. In response to Ruth's question, Boaz does not refer to any relationship. Rather, he tells her that she has earned his concern solely on her own merits through the report he has heard about her kindness and faithfulness to her mother-in-law. Though she is at the lowest rung of society, being unfortunate three times over (as a woman, a childless widow, and a foreigner), Boaz gives her her due worth as a person even in his patriarchal manner. Accepting her position in the patriarchal society, Ruth thanks Boaz in a subservient manner, recognizing herself as even lower than his maidservants as she says, "May I prove worthy of your favor, my lord. You have consoled your servant with your kind words, though I am not the equal of your maidservants" (2:13). Here the generous and noble character of Boaz shines forth in his response, actions, and recognition of Ruth's goodness. He goes beyond the demands of the law and societal expectations in letting her share in his meal and in instructing the harvesters to let her get in with them and even to drop some handfuls of grain for her (2:14-15).[22]

When Ruth returns to Naomi at the end of the day with about an *ephah* (or a bushel) of barley and her leftover food from lunch, Naomi eagerly questions her about the day's happenings (2:17-19). This homey conversation between the two women is quite realistic. It is here that Naomi learns at whose field Ruth has been gleaning. Although as readers we already know Boaz to be their kinsman, it is only at this point in the story that the two women make the connection (2:20). As readers, we can already imagine the women, especially Naomi, seeing the possibility of the levirate law being invoked in Ruth's case and an opportunity for them to be "redeemed" from their situation. Although the narrator does not yet make Naomi mention directly such a law, it is implied when she says to Ruth, "This man is a close relative, one with a right of redemption over us" (2:20b). According to Israel's law, it was the obligation of the nearest kin to redeem the land of a kinsman who was forced to relinquish his land because he had fallen into debt (Lev. 25:25). It seems implied from Naomi's statement that her husband Elimelech has land in Bethlehem. We can assume that Elimelech sold the land when they moved to Moab. Being poor and a woman at that, Naomi cannot redeem it herself. This is where Boaz enters the picture. Thus Boaz's identification as a kinsman will have a direct bearing on the resolution of the women's problems.

Practical woman that she is, Naomi gives Ruth prudent advice, hinting to her that it would be better for her to work in Boaz's field than to expose herself to harm by venturing into the fields of other landowners (2:22). Relying on her mother-in-law's practical wisdom, Ruth stays close to the prominent kinsman until the end of the wheat and barley harvest (2:23).

Third Chapter: Boaz Encounters Ruth (3:1-18)

This chapter is a model of artistic suspense in that the three major characters are projected as knowing how the story is supposed to develop.[23] Naomi has just identified Boaz and has begun thinking of him as a possible kinsman-redeemer. Before making the two widows act, the narrator makes them wait for the end of the harvest season and the time for winnowing the grain, usually a happy time for any landowner.

Ruth and Naomi are again together. A promising tomorrow dawns on Naomi, a widow beyond child-bearing age. Her only hope of security and prosperity for herself is through Ruth, who is still of child-bearing age. It is therefore understandable for her to show initiative and interest in Ruth's future, for her daughter-in-law's success will also be hers. She questions Ruth about her future and helps her find another husband, specifically Boaz (3:1-2a). She sends Ruth to Boaz's threshing floor where he is sleeping after giving her specific instructions to wash and perfume herself and to wear her finest clothes (3:2b-4). Although it is not clear precisely what Naomi has in mind, the sexual overtones of the incident cannot be ignored. We can easily construe this action as seduction even if the text does not explicitate it. The text implies that Naomi, in her advice to Ruth, is well aware of what might happen when Ruth lies at the feet of Boaz.

Ruth does what Naomi advised her to do. The narrator tells us that Ruth patiently waits until Boaz has eaten and drunk and lain down before she removes the mantle from his feet and lies down (3:5-7). The narrator's description sounds provocative, creating a certain tension within the reader. Laffey, in citing Campbell and Humbert, offers the following comments:

> The reference here to "feet" or "legs" is provocative — its cognate a euphemism for the penis — yet the term is deliberately ambiguous (Campbell). Ruth, who has sought food in the manner appropriate to widows, now, by this obvious but discreet gesture (Humbert) seeks a husband.[24]

Viviano comments further on the use of the term "feet." She writes:

> The compromising position into which Naomi sends Ruth is clear when one realizes that the term "feet" in Hebrew often refers to the male genitals. The double meaning may be intended to rouse the interest of the audience, "to raise a few eyebrows," only to show that the unusual steps taken by Ruth do not end up in an illicit sexual union, but reveal the honorable character of Boaz.[25]

The tension continues to build up until Boaz awakens in the middle of the night startled to find a woman there. The plot thickens and leads us to the next episode.

Boaz asks for the woman's identity. Here he no longer asks "whose" she is as in the first time he saw Ruth (2:5), but "who" she is (3:9a). This change in form is significant. By it, the author is either emphasizing that Ruth now has an identity which she previously lacked or that she belongs to no one and thereby is available for marriage. The implication here in the context of a patriarchal culture is that Boaz can now take her and make her "his own."[26] Consistent with her awareness of a woman's position at that time, she identifies herself not only by name but also by her subservient role in relation to Boaz, "I am Ruth, your servant."

With her new knowledge that Boaz is a kinsman-redeemer of Elimelech's family, she also goes further, asking Boaz to spread a corner of his garment over her (3:9b). When one says "spread the corner of your cloak over me," it is like saying "spread your wing over me." The words are meant to recall the protecting wing of Israel's God.[27] Ruth's intentions are more than romantic. She is literally asking Boaz to place her intimately under his protection and even into his possession.[28] Boaz responds by invoking God to bless her for her fidelity to the covenant. He comments that this act of loyalty to Israel's covenant, in seeking for herself not a young husband but an appropriate one, is greater than her first (an obvious reference to her loyalty to Naomi).

Boaz promises to do for her all that she asks. However, the narrator introduces a complication to the early solution of the problem and catches the characters at loose ends. He makes Boaz come out with an information to Ruth that he is not her closest kin. In other words, the protector was not just any relative, for there was a definite line of priority, although we do not know exactly how it worked then.[29] This gives us a sense of how women of that time, and of the present for that matter, have to go through an uphill battle in order to succeed.

Fortunately for Ruth, Boaz assures her that he will do what he can so she may be able to fulfill the levirate marriage, for she is, after all, a worthy woman. He does not take advantage of Ruth but agrees to take the necessary steps to marry her. He then tells Ruth to lie at his feet until morning. She does as she is told. Being an honorable man, Boaz further instructs Ruth to keep secret the fact that "a woman" had come to the threshing floor. It is entirely understandable that he would want to save Ruth from unnecessary scandal. He has to protect not only his reputation but also that of Ruth who, if found out to be sleeping with a man, could easily be accused and penalized heavily for immorality. Before she leaves, he gives her barley for her mother-in-law (3:14-15).

When Ruth returns home, Naomi greets her with a question, "How did you fare?" Having sent her daughter-in-law to Boaz in a compromising position, she is understandably curious as to what happened between them. The narrator summarizes that Ruth revealed to Naomi everything she wanted to know but quotes Boaz's words to her about not going back to her mother-in-law empty-handed. Naomi responds with confidence, but the narrator does not tell us why. What will happen next? Here we are left in suspense for a while.

As we read through this chapter, we see how women, in order to achieve their goals, are oftentimes left with no other choice but to take a compromising position vis-à-vis men. Inferior to man, the biblical woman always had to negotiate from a position of weakness and dependence. Although today's woman has come a long way from the woman of biblical times, much remains to be desired until women and men can come to regard one another as equally sharing the same humanity and the same opportunities in life.

Fourth Chapter: The Resolution and Conclusion of Story

This chapter opens with Boaz waiting for the arrival of the unnamed kinsman-redeemer. Upon his arrival at the town gate, the redemption and marriage negotiations begin. The narrator then gives us a description of the proceedings, which correspond to what we know of biblical times—but there are specific difficulties on our part because we do not know enough (4:1-2).[30] All that is clear to us is that a quorum of the town's elders have to convene and witness the negotiations. In typical patriarchal fashion the subject matter of the negotiations is not the women relatives, Naomi and Ruth, but rather the dead man Elimelech's property (4:3).[31] Boaz informs the unnamed relative that he is first in line to acquire the land. But Boaz also tells the unnamed relative that if he chooses to renege on his right, he, Boaz, himself will redeem the land.

To have a better understanding of this text, let us consider two general laws[32] involved in the case under negotiation. In ancient society, property was to remain in the hands of the same tribal or familial members. If it was lost for whatever reasons, the relative-protector had to help get it back. The second law involved levirate marriage which made possible the perpetuation of a patriarchal line in those families where the husband died before his wife had conceived any offspring.[33] Because the ancient Israelites did not believe in life after death, the only way to continue one's existence after death was through one's children. To be sonless in Israel meant that one would cease to exist. To prevent this tragedy, the levirate law was applied which specified that if the husband died before begetting a son, a brother-in-law or some other relative was to marry the widow and have a son in the name of the deceased as a recognition of his obligation to continue the family line. Although this was the law's implicit way of providing for the widow, undoubtedly the pressure was always on the woman in that she had to provide a descendant for her dead husband. In the Bible's patriarchal context, her faithfulness to God's law was always linked to her conscientiousness or resourcefulness in so providing. Tamar is an example of this kind of faithfulness. She was a Canaanite outsider left childless by the death of her first and second husbands, both sons of Judah. When Judah failed to do his duty in providing her as her husband with a third son, she disguised herself as a prostitute and seduced him. Only later did she reveal that Judah was the father, when he discovered his widowed daughter-in-law in a pregnant situation that he regarded as scandalous, causing him to recognize that she was more just and faithful to God's law than he was.[34] In Ruth's story, both she and her widowed mother-in-law show resourcefulness in securing Boaz's cooperation to fulfill the levirate law.

However, with regard to land ownership the conditions under which women could own land in a patriarchal society are somewhat nebulous. But in the case of Naomi and Ruth, the two general laws may be applicable. The relative-protector has to help Naomi get back Elimelech's property, and, since as a woman she has no right to have it under her name, a close relative will have to be willing to redeem and own it for her. In order to ensure that the property will be kept in the same family, it is important to have male heirs. This is where the levirate law would be applicable to Ruth, since she is still of child-bearing age.

Boaz's next response to the closest relative considers these general laws. In fairness to the unnamed relative, Boaz further informs him that his obligation is not only to redeem the property but also to fulfill the levirate law by taking the widow who is part of the man's property (4:5). The widow referred to here should be Naomi, but since she is beyond child-bearing age, Ruth will have to be the bride.[35] The unnamed kinsman is willing to redeem the land but for some reason is unwilling or unable to marry Ruth, perhaps because of the possibility of his losing whatever economic advantage the land represents if Ruth will have children claiming the land as their inheritance (4:6).[36] This new detail changes the equation of things. It is one thing to buy land and to be given the first option to do so as a close relative of the deceased, but it is quite another thing to realize that the land will ultimately belong to the son whom one will raise for the deceased.[37] The position of this close relative is well taken. Understandably no criticism is leveled against him for his rejection of his right of redemption. This leads us to only one person who is clearly the intended redeemer in this story — Boaz himself.

The transaction is thereby legalized in the presence of the elders. As a transition narrative, we are given a description of a strange custom when an agreement between the negotiating parties is reached (4:9-10). Instead of a written document as is practiced today, each negotiating party removes his sandals and gives it to the other, with the elders publicly testifying as witnesses to the contract (4:11).[38] After the witnessing ceremony, they all bless Ruth, wishing her many offspring.

Conclusion: A Child Is Born to Ruth (4:13-17)

The elders' blessing comes to fulfillment. The union between Ruth and Boaz is immediately blessed with a child. Naomi's emptiness in the beginning of the book is filled at the end of the story. The famine that accentuated the beginning of the story is now significantly replaced by an abundant harvest. Emptiness becomes fullness. A curse turns into a blessing.

The women of Israel joyfully turn to Naomi and proclaim
Yahweh for providing her with an heir and a faithful daughter-
in-law:

Blessed be Yahweh who has provided you today with an
heir. May he become famous in Israel! He will be your
comfort and stay in your old age, for he is born of a daughter-in-law who loves you and is worth more than seven
sons.

At first glance, it would seem as if the blessing belongs only
to Naomi since the women of Israel assign the heir as belonging
to her, not to Ruth, the real mother. The women of the neighborhood even exclaim, "A son has been born for Naomi!" Then
the women continue to name the boy (4:17). It is rather strange
that the right to name the child is not given to the father in
accordance with the patriarchal custom. If the women should
be given this unexpected privilege to name the boy, why not give
it to both Ruth and Naomi, the child's mother and grandmother,
respectively? Although from a feminist perspective this seems
like a great improvement, it is difficult for us to understand this
deviation from patriarchal custom. One commentator says that
perhaps the context in which the neighbor women name the boy
was the celebration of his blessed birth; pronouncing the boy's
name was evidently a way of congratulating Naomi.[39] If such was
the case, we continue to feel for Ruth, who, in spite of her
faithfulness in embracing Israel's law, is not even congratulated.
She appears to be left out in the story's glorious ending.

From the women's words, it would also seem that Ruth is
merely used for Naomi's advantage — so that she may have an
heir and so that her curse will be turned into a blessing. This is
partly understandable because as a foreigner the only way Ruth
will have an identity and right in Israel is through the lineage
of Naomi's husband. Therefore the women's words are in keeping with Israel's laws and traditions. However, they do recognize
her great worth as a person when in their blessing to Naomi
they say of the child, "for he is born of a daughter-in-law who
loves you and is worth more than seven sons." In the patriarchal
context, "to be worth more than seven sons" is one of the highest

praises given to any woman in the Old Testament. Ruth is truly this kind of woman. The women themselves see in her more than just her child-bearing capacity. They recognize in her a great capacity for love.

The story ends with a genealogy (4:18-22) which is rather curious because for all the care the writer takes in invoking the levirate law so that Elimelech and Mahlon's lineage may continue, neither of them is mentioned. Instead the genealogy recognizes Boaz and not Mahlon as the father of Obed, Ruth's firstborn son. Obed becomes the father of Jesse, who is the father of King David and from whose lineage the Christ comes.

However, even if Ruth remains unrecognized in the Old Testament lineage,[40] it is believed that oral tradition has preserved her as David's great-grandmother. This tradition has been carried through to the New Testament era. The genealogy that opens Matthew's Gospel unexpectedly mentions her along with three other women, all of whom are outsiders: Tamar, the Canaanite childless widow of Judah's two sons; Rahab, the Canaanite harlot whose kindness in protecting the Israelite spies made the conquest of Jericho possible (chapter 2 of this book); and Bathsheba (although unnamed, is recognized only through her pious husband Uriah, a Hittite, whom David conspired to kill; she was a victim of David's lust).[41] All these four women, though foreigners, are acknowledged for their steadfastness to Israel's law. Thus Ruth's inclusion in the New Testament genealogy recognizes her and not her Israelite in-laws as the one faithful to the law in raising up a child to her dead husband. Through her faithfulness, Ruth made herself available as God's creative instrument in continuing the line of the Messiah.

IMAGES OF FAITH AND SPIRITUALITY

After reading and re-reading Ruth's story, one can't help but realize how pregnant it is with images and movements of faith and spirituality. These images are present not only in Ruth as a person but also in the two other main characters, Naomi and Boaz. God's presence in the story is manifested through the blessings and oaths that are spoken by the main characters, by the elders and Israelite neighbor women. It is through the actions and faith of the main characters that God's presence is incarnated and the divine blessings are realized.

In the story, God is also seen as the principal cause of all that happens, both good and bad. God causes the famine to happen and to end. God is the cause of Naomi's emptiness and misery, as well as the source of her abundance at the end of the story. Nonetheless God's presence is reflected as challenges to growth in the movements of life transitions experienced by the women characters, especially in their experiences of good-byes and self-emptying. God is present all throughout, as mediated in the lives and events of those who are faithful to the covenant. Since Ruth's story is interwoven in the lives of both Naomi and Boaz, we shall look at the spiritual legacies left us by these three characters.

Faith and the Experience of Emptiness in Life Transitions

The contrast between emptiness and fullness runs through the entire book. This is seen not only in the setting itself but also in the lives of the women characters. The famine or the emptiness of the land that sets the story in motion drives Naomi's family to seek "greener pastures." Leaving one's country and culture is an experience of emptying akin to an experience of loss—not only loss of food in time of famine but also loss of relationships and of property and land. To a certain extent, it recalls a recurring motif in the life of Israel and all throughout salvation history that began with God inviting Abraham to leave his clan and his ancestral home for a promised land. In Abraham we saw that God's promise and blessing are indissolubly bound up with a departure, an emptying of anything that prevents one from setting out on an adventure with God. But for Naomi, Moab did not turn out to be a land of promise but a place of emptiness. There she lost not only her husband but later her two sons as well. Her emptiness seemed irreparable, her life so hollow deep within. Like the psalmist, these words could have echoed in Naomi's heart: "How could we sing a song to the Lord in a foreign land?" (Ps. 137:4, NAB).

It would be difficult indeed for anyone in Naomi's predicament to sing a song to God when feeling so alienated from God, life, others, and even self. Based on our human experience, our capacity to pray is greatly influenced by what we experience in our body and spirit. We also know that grief has a way of devouring our spiritual life, leaving us in the desert to feel parched, empty, depleted, lonely, and alienated.

Naomi could attribute the cause of her incurable emptiness only to God ("Yahweh's hand has been raised against me!" — 1:13c). Thus only God could fill it. Beyond her empty feeling and sense of God's absence is perhaps a fragile hope that God will also cause her misery to cease. Perhaps this was in her mind and heart when the narrator says:

> Having heard that Yahweh had come to help his [sic] people by giving them food, Naomi prepared to return home (1:9).

In her poverty her emptiness is so basic — expressed only in her hunger for food. But perhaps beyond this need to fill her physical hunger is a keen desire to reconcile herself with the past, to catch a glimpse of home and the possibility of who she is meant to be. John Dunne once wrote:[42]

> At every turn in the road
> a new illuminating is needed to find the way
> and a new kindling is needed to follow the way.

Dunne seems to speak here of moments of transition in one's life when one needs to search within to find illumination or guidance to continue going forward on the road to life. This search within one's self essentially involves the movement to return to the past — to one's home and roots — and to be reconciled with it.

Naomi, in her poverty and emptiness, thinks of home not only as a place where she could experience God's blessing again ("having heard that Yahweh had come to help his [sic] people") but also as a place where she can find peace and acceptance of her painful situation ("Don't call me Naomi. Call me Mara for Yahweh has made life bitter for me"). This movement is reflective of a deep longing that is present in every human heart. A part in us is always yearning, longing, and quietly crying out for the true homeland where life is no longer painful and unfair.[43]

Undoubtedly Naomi's two Moabite daughters-in-law are also experiencing emptiness and grief at losing their husbands. In their loss, their initial response is to cling to what is familiar (to continue living with Naomi and to remain in her clan) even if it does not seem to give them any kind of future. Orpah is practical-minded in dealing with her emptiness. In spite of the pain of saying good-bye to her relationships (with Naomi and Ruth) and to what has already become familiar to her, she heeds Naomi's advice and returns to her "mother's house." Perhaps she realized that life could still offer her a future in her own homeland. Or perhaps she also caught a glimpse of home and the possibility of who she could still become.

Companionship in Time of Transition

On the other hand, Ruth clings to her mother-in-law and takes a risk of embracing her, her land, and her God even if the future is uncertain and seemingly bleak. Although she too is going through transition, she offers Naomi her presence and companionship. She feels for her mother-in-law because she too knows the pain of loss and the difficulty of adjusting to a new reality. But unlike Naomi, she is not allowing this life transition to discourage or embitter her. For her the movement back to her mother's house seems to be a movement away from what and who she is meant to be. Instead she follows the movement of Israel's first patriarch by leaving her homeland and venturing into the unknown. Like Abraham, she departs from her homeland and empties herself of anything that prevents her from setting out on an adventure with Abraham's and Naomi's God. But unlike Abraham, the God of Israel does not appear to her with a promise and a blessing. She has none of these assurances. She leaves relying only on Naomi's God and the strength of her love for her mother-in-law. She deals with her emptiness by further emptying herself so she can embrace totally the God of Abraham, of Naomi, and of Israel. She lets go of the past in order to embrace the future with great faithfulness. And in these beautiful words which have become an immortal prayer of fidelity, she accompanies Naomi through her life transition:

> 'Wherever you go, I will go,
> wherever you live, I will live.
> Your people shall be my people,
> and your God, my God.
> Wherever you die, I will die
> and there I will be buried.
> May Yahweh do this thing to me
> and more also,
> if even death should come between us!' (1:16-17, JB).

Blessing Prayers

God's presence permeates the entire story in the blessings and oaths that are spoken and invoked by the main characters. It begins with Naomi blessing her two daughters-in-law and ends with the women of Bethlehem blessing Naomi for the birth of Ruth's son, Obed. Before discussing each blessing prayer, let us therefore look at blessing not just as a form of prayer but as a word of grace and a gift of life.

Practically every book of the Bible contains one or several blessings. The word or act of blessing is understood as the bestowal of divine favor, the giving of praise and thanksgiving to God, and the invocation of divine favor for a person.[44] It has as its basic principle God's gracious or favorable will toward us. Blessing is a gift that touches life and its mystery. But it is also *word* as much as *gift*, speaking as much as good because the good it carries with it is not a precise object or definite gift because it belongs not to the sphere of *having* but of *being* and because it stresses not the action of a human being but the creation of God.[45]

Naomi Blesses Ruth and Orpah. The first of many blessings is the one that comes forth from Naomi's emptiness. She prays for God's kindness to fall upon her two widowed daughters-in-law as she urges them to go back to their mothers' houses:

". . . may Yahweh be kind to you, as you have been to your dead and to me. May [Yahweh] also grant each of you rest in the home of another husband" (1:8).

The blessing includes her daughters-in-law's past and their future. For the past, Naomi's blessing expresses her thanksgiving for her daughters-in-law's kindness to her and to their late husbands. For the future, her blessing consists of two parts. First, she prays that they may find happiness and fulfillment as mothers. This is very much in keeping with woman's position in ancient society where her worth and fulfillment were inextricably connected to her child-bearing and rearing capacities and obligation. The second part flows from the first. Here Naomi prays that they find happiness and "rest" in their future husbands. The concept of "rest" is implied when a woman fulfills her role as wife and mother. This gives a woman a sense of "being settled" or "being at rest" in one's expected role in life.

Boaz Blesses Ruth. The second and third blessings come from Boaz's lips. The first was given when Ruth wondered why she, as a foreigner, should be favored by him (2:10). Boaz responds by praising her for her kindness and fidelity to her mother-in-law. Then he pronounces a blessing upon her. However, he does this like a father to a daughter, which was a common form of blessing in biblical times. Fathers would bless their sons or daughters as a way of affirming their good behavior. Here Boaz blesses Ruth in these words:

"May Yahweh reward you for this [referring to Ruth's loyalty to her mother-in-law]! May you receive full recompense from Yahweh, the God of Israel, under whose wings you have come for refuge!" (2:10).

Just as Naomi asked God to bless her daughters-in-law (1:8-9), so now Boaz asks Yahweh's blessings for Ruth, who has taken refuge under the protective wings of the God of Israel. In the blessing, Boaz goes beyond mere recognition of Ruth's human kindness and acknowledges her great act of faith in embracing Israel's God ("under whose wings you have come for refuge!"). This is a foreshadowing of how Ruth would put this blessing prayer into action when later, at Boaz's threshing floor, she asks him to spread the corner of his cloak over her. Literally she is saying to him, "spread your wing over me," recalling the protective wing of Israel's God. Boaz responds with another blessing. This time he blesses her for her greater act of kindness in being faithful to the covenant, particularly the levirate law, in his reference to Ruth's not going after young men:

> "May Yahweh bless you, my daughter! This kindness of yours now is even greater than that which you have shown earlier, for you have not gone after young men, rich or poor . . ." (3:10).

The Elders and Other Witnesses at the City Gate Bless Ruth through Boaz. The fourth blessing is after the legalization of the marriage and redemption negotiation between Boaz and Naomi's closest kin. The elders and other witnesses of the legal action break into a song of blessing. However, the blessing is not addressed directly to Ruth but to Boaz. In fact, she is not mentioned at all by name but is only referred to as the "woman." Perhaps this is to emphasize that she will always be a foreigner in spite of her conversion to Israel's faith, and as a woman and foreigner she will always belong to society's inferior class. The manner in which the elders and people pronounce their blessing is also very much in keeping with patriarchy. It recalls the family lineage which they pray would prosper through the application of the levirate law. Surprisingly they name some of the women of Israel's history, specifically Rachel, Leah, and Tamar, who had continued the lineage and built up Israel's house. But expectedly these women are simply recognized for providing many offspring. Here are their words:

> ". . . May Yahweh make the *woman* coming into your house like Rachel and Leah, who together built up the house of Israel. May you prosper in Ephrathah and be of good standing in Bethlehem. And through the offspring Yahweh will give you by the *woman,* may your house become like that of Perez whom Tamar bore to Judah" (4:11b-12).[46]

The Women Bless Naomi. The last of the blessings comes at the final scene of the story. The women pronounce a blessing on Naomi to praise and thank God for filling her emptiness. Now that she has a descendant through Ruth, her emptiness is full. The emptiness which sets the scene of the story is now reversed. Naomi regains her original identity as "pleasant." No longer is she Mara, "the bitter one." The women who saw her affliction when she returned to Bethlehem rejoice with her, for her curse has now turned into blessing. They say to her:

> "Blessed be Yahweh who has provided you today with an heir. May he become famous in Israel! He will be your comfort and stay in your old age, for he is born of a daughter-in-law who loves you and is worth more than seven sons" (4:14-15).

Faith as Fidelity

The theme of fidelity is like a thread that runs through the entire story, subtly connecting to God the characters' words, actions, and relationships with one another. This biblical fidelity (in Hebrew, *hesed*) is "loyalty born of covenant bonding."[47] It is implied, if not explicitly mentioned, in all the blessing prayers pronounced by the main characters as well as by the elders, witnesses, and women of Bethlehem.

Biblical fidelity recalls the faith of Israel that began with the departure of Abraham and ended with a covenant with God. It remembers the unique friendship established between God and Israel that is echoed in the entire book and exemplified by Ruth and the other characters of the story—they are God's people, and Yahweh is their God. At the very heart of this covenant fidelity is their faith that Yahweh is the God of life and therefore would call them to greater life.

But how can we translate this covenant fidelity into today's language and setting? Is it still relevant to us in our contemporary world when everything seems temporary and short-lived?

If the core of covenant fidelity is the faith that Yahweh, the living God, calls each of us to greater life, then its deep message is ageless. When we reflect on our human tendencies, we are easily led toward the path of darkness and self-destruction. Faith calls us out of our sinful tendency and invites us to face the light and to choose life. Faith moves us to break away from anything that stunts our growth as persons and invites us to look forward to a fuller life ahead. "Faith enables us to look upon each 'letting go' with optimism and it prepares us to face other more painful relinquishments which commit us more fully to God's service."[48] It leads us to fuller life and enables us to catch a glimpse of who we are meant to be. Like Ruth and Naomi, faith urges us to move forward and embrace the God of life.

In the following section, let us apply some of the insights we have gained through our discussion on prayer and spirituality and allow Ruth and Naomi to guide us in our ongoing reflection on life. Let us also look at the figures of Ruth and Naomi in today's world and permit them to challenge our faith.

THE RUTH AND NAOMI OF TODAY

We continue to see the figures of Ruth and Naomi today in the many women who go through various kinds of painful and difficult life transitions—transitions from being a wife to being a widow, from being married to being divorced or separated, from being financially stable to being poor, from having a home to being homeless. We see them in the faces of the poor, the frustrated, the unfulfilled, the women abandoned by their husbands, and those in grief. We also see them in the women who try to overcome obstacles in their homes, in their places of work, and in foreign countries.

On one hand, Ruth's figure is more prominent in the women who labor day and night in fields, factories, market places, offices, and in unexpected places of work in order to provide food and other basic necessities for themselves and their families. We also see her in the women who loyally sacrifice themselves on the altar of the home for the sake of their children's future or as companions to their aged or sick parents.

On the other hand, we see Naomi's presence in the grandmothers who provide practical guidance to their daughters and grandchildren—grandmothers who become surrogate mothers to their grandchildren while the children's parents work for the sustenance and survival of the entire family. We see her in the retired worker who has to survive on a fixed but meager pension. We see her in the embittered old women who have resigned themselves to their poverty. She is in the women who are going through crises of mid-life or of aging. We see her faithfully sitting at the church steps waiting for alms or selling candles. Both she and Ruth are ever present in our world. If we but open our eyes wide enough, we will not miss their presence in our homes and society today.

Thus the figures of Ruth and Naomi seem to leap out of the pages of the Bible in the lives of today's women. One of these women is Munda, who had to take up the multiple roles of mother, father, and breadwinner of the family when her husband abandoned her for another woman. In her strong belief that their poverty could be alleviated by leaving their hometown in the Philippine countryside, Munda, a peasant mother of six, decided to try her luck in the city. In her hometown, she supported her family as a sugar farm worker, but her meager income was not even enough to buy food for her children. They could eat only two square meals a day during the harvest season, while during the rest of the year they could eat scarcely one square meal a day.

She had heard that in the city jobs were plenty. Together with her brood of six she ventured into the city, using whatever little she had gathered for their transportation by selling everything they owned, leaving only the clothes on their backs. But she heard wrong. No job was available for anyone with her background. With all her resources gone, she and her children ended up begging for food at the steps of the cathedral. The women candle vendors along the cathedral entrance took pity on her and helped her get started to vend candles with them. One of the women lent her a small amount to sell her own candles. With a daily capital of thirty-five pesos (approximately US $1.40), she would buy the necessary materials to make her own candles to sell for the day. She would be very happy if she could make a profit of forty pesos a day because that would assure her that her family would not go hungry for the day.

Having no place to live, Munda and her children sleep on the sidewalks or on the church steps. Fortunately, two of her elder daughters and a son, ranging in age from eleven to sixteen, have been sheltered at the home for street children. For Munda, this kind of existence is much better than what they used to have in the sugar fields. She is not bitter at all. She could live with her present insecurity, knowing that God would take pity on her as she prays and sells candles at the doorsteps of the cathedral. Waiting for devotees to buy candles and being requested by devotees to pray for their intentions have given her a sense of mission in life. She believes that no matter how poor and illiterate she is, God will listen to her humble prayer, as God did when they first came to the city. So, day and night she sits at the church steps, hoping that people will stop to buy candles for her to light before the Child Jesus for their various intentions. People do stop. And with every candle she lights, her simple prayer, coming from a pure and humble faith, is lifted up to the heavens.

A more poignant image of today's Ruth is reflected in the life of Tising, a widow and mother of five. She lives in the slums dotting the seaport area of Cebu City. Her husband used to support their family from his meager income as a *cargador* or cargo worker at the pier. But two years ago tragedy befell Tising's family. Her husband was killed in a freak accident while he was unloading cargo from a ship. A loosely secured ton of cargo fell on him, crushing him to death. He had no insurance, for he was only a casual worker. Since then Tising has had to become a full-time breadwinner, taking up odd jobs simply to survive. Her eldest son, who is eighteen years old, brings in an additional amount from his occasional job as a *cargador* while two elder daughters between the ages of thirteen and sixteen are helping her sell lottery tickets and cigarettes. Still there are many days during the week when they do not have enough to eat, for their combined income is oftentimes spent for the medication of Tising's youngest son, who has recently been diagnosed as having a rare liver ailment.

To assure that her family will have food daily, she goes to the pier twice or thrice a week to wait, along with other poor women and children, for the arrival of cargo ships carrying grain from the provinces. It usually happens that as the sacks of rice are unloaded from the ships, one or two sacks break, spilling some of their contents. After the unloading, the cargo workers allow the poor people waiting around to collect the spilled grain. In the rush, if Tising is fast enough to get there ahead of the others, she could collect enough to feed her family for one or two days. Sometimes others get there ahead of her and she comes home empty-handed. On occasion, if there are no broken sacks, the *cargadores* themselves bore a few holes in one or several of the sacks so that grain can fall on the ground for their wives or children to collect. In a sense, the poor are helping one another survive. Such a poignant plight of today's poor women and children reminds us always of Israel's poor and of the world's poor who have to continually scrounge for food simply to survive.

In spite of her poverty, Tising never seems to falter in her faith and hope in God. In fact she clings to her faith even more. Although her faith is somewhat fatalistic, there is a simplicity in it that makes one feel God's presence in her attitude of total trust and confidence in divine deliverance and care.

PRAYING WITH RUTH

Suggestions for Prayer and Reflection

• Reflect on the following questions: What stirred within me as I read and re-read Ruth's story and the plight of today's women like her? Do I see any connection between her situation and those of today's Ruths? In what ways can I identify with Ruth? What are my feelings and realizations?

(Pause for silent reflection. If applicable, share your reflections on the above questions with a group during a faith-sharing session. If you are doing an individual recollection or reflection, it would be helpful to write down some of your feelings and insights in your journal.)

• After the reflection or sharing, allow the images of today's Ruths to fill your consciousness and in silence lift them up to God.

• Then make the following *Prayer of Solidarity*[49] your own while adding your own verses to it if necessary:

> We believe in the goodness and value of women:
> our strength and our willingness to weep;
> our capacity to support each other, instead of being
>   rivals;
> our ability to cope with children's demands and the
>   burdens of life;
> our willingness and ability to get on with the job;
> our spirituality and our earthiness, flowing with life,
>   birth, and death.
>
> We affirm the story of women as the story of human-
>   kind:
> food gatherers and farmers
> child rearers and teachers
> pioneers and policy makers
> needleworkers and textile makers
> homemakers and factory workers
> parents, scientists, doctors
> housekeepers and economists
> givers of life and creators of art and thought
> unpaid hidden workers at home and paid members
>   of the work force outside.
> We rejoice in our diversity and versatility,
> our intuition and our logic.
>
> We confess our failures, frailties, and imperfection,
> including our past acceptance of violence and injus-
>   tice
> in relationships between women and men.
>
> We look forward to the future in faith and hope,
> working for the day when we and all our sisters
> no longer have to fit a stereotype
> but are free to use all our gifts
> and to share in all the benefits of human life and
>   work

when violence is banished,
both women and men are able to love and to be
      loved,
and the work and wealth of our world is justly shared.

We believe that our future depends on us,
but that all the forces for good, love, peace, and
      justice,
all the creative powers of the universe,
work with us to achieve that vision.
May it come soon.
Amen.

—Ann Wansbrough

• *Prayer in Action.* Concretize your prayer by engaging in the
following actions:
 — Be involved in a feeding program for the urban poor.
 — Support the cooperative programs in some of the poor
   areas.
 — Join women's organizations or groups that are helping alle-
   viate poverty, especially in urban or rural poor areas.
 — Help out a poor widow who is the "food gatherer" for the
   family.
 — Be present to someone who is grieving.

PRAYING WITH NAOMI

Suggestions for Prayer and Reflection

• Read and re-read the first chapter of the Book of Ruth until
you get a mental picture of Naomi and her situation. Then
reflect on the following questions: What moved or stirred within
me as I read her story? What particular images of today's Naomi
surface on my consciousness? Have there been instances or
experiences in my life when I felt like Naomi—spent, bitter,
alienated, abandoned, and empty inside?

(Pause for silent reflection, then do some journaling if it
helps.)

• *Prayer of Lament and Solidarity.* In silence read slowly the following prayer, saying each line as if it were your own as you think of today's Naomis or as you express your own experience of emptiness. (Be aware of what stirs within you while and after praying the prayer of lament. Write your thoughts and feelings in your journal if it helps.):

> Remember Yahweh, what has befallen me,
> Look, and see my disgrace . . .
> I am like an orphan,
> fatherless and widowed . . .
>
> With the yoke stifling my breath,
> without rest I work to death . . .
>
> I brave the desert heat and the sword
> just to get hard-earned food.
>
> My skin is hot, as with fever,
> dried up
> and shriveled by hunger.
>
> From my heart joy is gone;
> I danced then,
> but now I lament.
>
> Why then should you abandon me, O God?
> Why forget me for so long a time?
> Lead me to you again, O God,
> that I may be restored;
> renew my days as of old.
> (Adapted from Lam. 5:1,3,5,10,15,17,20,21)

• *Prayer in Action.* Concretize your prayer by engaging in the following actions:

— Listen and be present to someone who is going through grief or life transition.

(If you are going through some kind of difficult transition

yourself, share with someone your journey. Seek out a spiritual companion who can guide you.)
— Join a women's support group (if there's one in your neighborhood) in which the members help one another go through difficult life transitions. Or get together with your friends who are undergoing similar experiences of transition.
— Attend a seminar on life transition.
— Help out a poor and lonely old widow in the neighborhood or in the slums.

• *For further reading and reflection.* Read *Praying Our Goodbyes* by Joyce Rupp, O.S.M. (Quezon City, Philippines: Claretian Publications, 1990).

5

ABIGAIL

An Advocate of Pacifism

As we read the pages of the Old Testament, especially the Deuteronomic books,[1] we realize that in ancient times war was endemic. Its presence in the world of the Bible allows revelation to articulate an essential element of the mystery in which humanity is engaged and of which salvation is the largesse in the combat between God or the forces of good and Satan or the forces of evil.[2] To a certain extent, the inclusion of war and violence in the sacred pages of the Bible is understandable because the ancient Eastern peoples did not only transfer to the religious domain the results of their social experience but also introduced war into its representation of the divine world.[3] Although Israel cut short the polytheism of its neighbors, it preserved the polytheist's image of a combatant God. It simply transformed the imagery to adapt to monotheism and to give it a place in the earthly realization of God's plan.[4] Thus, in many scriptural texts where the God of Israel is projected as a liberator, it is usually accompanied by violent images, tales of war and victory. Israel's ancient name for God is "Lord God of

Hosts" (YHWH Sabaoth), an allusion either to the armies of heaven or to the warriors of Israel.[5]

Israel had to engage in battles in order to claim Canaan, the land God promised to its ancestors. Israel also believed that God sanctioned the extermination of Canaan because of its corrupted civilization made worse by a worship of the forces of nature (Deut. 7).[6] But since Israel got the land back by force, it also had to preserve it by force. The Israelites believed that God would always fight with them and would always be on their side for as long as they would be faithful to the covenant God had established with them as a people. Thus Israel's national wars would become "Yahweh's wars," and in defending its independence against foreign aggressors, Israel at the same time would be defending God's cause.[7] But only Yahweh could effect a victory—a victory over evil. Israel's victory belongs primarily to Yahweh. However, the fact that the inspired author of Scripture saw God's hand in the bleak events of war and battle in no way implies a divine justification for war in general or for any particular war. We can still discover God's message even in the midst of this ugly reality.[8]

The story of Abigail is presented to us in the First Book of Samuel, during the period of Israel's war of national liberation in which Saul and David were engaged. It is placed amidst the two encounters between Saul and David (chapters 24 and 26). Saul was still the anointed king of Israel at this time, but Yahweh has been displeased with him. Saul had earlier shown suspicion that David might be a rival for the throne (18:6-9). David, on the other hand, had shown a lot of promise as Israel's future king, and Yahweh seemed to be showing him favor. In the meantime, Saul had grown envious of David's popularity and military success. Out of jealousy and fear of losing his throne, Saul had wanted to kill David. David's encounter with Abigail happened at the time he was fleeing Saul and after the death of the prophet Samuel. Thus the story serves as a romantic interlude amidst the harsh realities of war and the characters' vulnerability to violence.

ABIGAIL'S STORY IN THE BIBLE

[1] The day Samuel died, all Israel gathered together to mourn him; after which they buried him at his home in Ramah.

Then David went down to the desert of Maon. ² A very rich man, owner of three thousand sheep and a thousand goats, lived there and had his farm in Carmel.

³ This man was named Nabal; his wife, Abigail. The woman was intelligent and beautiful; but the man himself, a Calebite, was rough and ill-mannered. He was at the time shearing his sheep in Carmel.

⁴ When David heard in the desert that Nabal was shearing his sheep, ⁵ he sent ten young men to the farm with this instruction, "Go to Nabal in Carmel and greet him for me ⁶ in these words: peace be with you and your family; peace be with all that is yours. ⁷ I heard that you have shearers with you. Now when your shepherds were with us, we did not harm them; neither did they miss anything while they were in Carmel. ⁸ Ask your servants and they will tell. So be kind to my servants since we come on a festive day; please give them and your son David whatever you can."

⁹ When David's young men arrived, they delivered this message to Nabal in David's name and then waited. ¹⁰ But Nabal answered David's servants, "Who is David? Who is the son of Jesse? Many nowadays are the servants who run away from their masters. ¹¹ Must I take my bread, my wine, my meat which I have slaughtered for my shearers and give it to men who come from I don't know where?" ¹² At this, David's young men left and returned to him, reporting everything Nabal had said. ¹³ David then said to his men, "Let every man strap on his sword!" And every one of them, including David, strapped on his sword. About four hundred men followed David while two hundred remained with the baggage.

¹⁴ One of Nabal's servants told Abigail, his wife, "David sent messengers from the desert to greet our master but he shouted at them. ¹⁵ Yet these men were very good to us. We suffered no harm and did not miss anything while we were living among them during our stay in the open country. ¹⁶ They were like a wall for us night and day while we were tending the sheep in their midst. ¹⁷ Now think over what you should do; for our master and his entire

family are surely doomed to die, but he is so wicked no one can speak to him."

[18] Abigail hurriedly prepared two hundred loaves, two skins of wine, five dressed sheep, five measures of roasted grain, a hundred cakes of pressed raisins, and two hundred cakes of pressed figs and loaded them on asses. [19] Then she said to her servants, "Go on ahead and I shall follow you." But she told her husband nothing of this.

[20] As she rode down the mountain on her ass, David and his men were coming down from the other direction. When she met them, [21] David was reflecting, "It was useless guarding all that this fellow has in the desert. Although he lost nothing belonging to him, he has returned me evil for good. [22] May God do so to David and more if by morning I leave a single male alive among those who belong to him."

[23] On seeing David, Abigail quickly dismounted from the ass and threw herself on the ground before him. [24] As she fell at his feet she said, "My lord, let the blame be on me! Let your handmaid speak to you; listen to her words. [25] Let not my lord pay attention to this ill-mannered man, Nabal, for he is just what his name says: he is a fool. I, your handmaid, did not see the young men whom you sent.

[26] Now, my lord, as Yahweh lives and as you live, it is Yahweh who prevents you from shedding blood and avenging yourself. Let your enemies and those who seek to harm my lord become like Nabal! [27]And now let this present which I have brought you, my lord, be given to the young men who follow you, [28] and please forgive me.

Yahweh will certainly give you a lasting family because you are fighting the battles of Yahweh and no evil shall be found in you as long as you live. [29] Should anyone make an attempt on your life, may the life of my lord be bound in the bundle of the living in the care of Yahweh, your God. May he hurl away the lives of your enemies as from the hollow of a sling.

[30] So when Yahweh fulfills his promises and appoints you as commander over Israel, [31] you shall have no reason to grieve or to feel any grief or regret for having unrightfully shed blood or taken revenge yourself. May Yahweh

bless you, and you, my lord, remember your handmaid."

[32] David then said to Abigail, "Blessed be Yahweh, the God of Israel, who sent you to meet me today! [33] Blessed be your good judgment and may you yourself be blessed, for you have prevented me from shedding blood and avenging myself today! [34] For as Yahweh, the God of Israel, lives, he has prevented me from hurting you. If you did not hurry to meet me, not a single male belonging to Nabal would have been alive by morning." [35] David accepted what she had brought him and told her, "Go back home in peace. I have listened to you and granted your request."

[36] Abigail went back to Nabal and found him holding a feast in his house.

He was joyful and very drunk so Abigail did not mention anything to him until the following day. [37] When morning came and Nabal had slept it off, his wife spoke to him about all these things. On hearing it Nabal had a stroke and remained paralyzed. [38] Ten days later, Yahweh let him die.

[39] When David heard that Nabal was dead, he said, "Blessed be Yahweh who has avenged the insult I received at the hand of Nabal and has prevented me from doing wrong. Yahweh himself has made Nabal's wrongdoings fall on his own head."

[40] David then sent his servants to Abigail in Carmel to propose marriage to her saying, "David has sent us to you to say that he wants you to be his wife." [41] Rising and bowing to the ground, Abigail answered, "May I be as a slave to wash the feet of my lord's servants." [42]She quickly rose and mounted an ass and, attended by five of her servants, she left with David's messengers and became his wife.

[43] David also married Ahinoam of Jezreel, making both her and Abigail his wives. [44] Saul, in the meantime, had given Michal, his daughter and David's wife, to Palti, son of Laish who was from Gallim.

A RE-READING OF ABIGAIL'S STORY

Abigail's story is presented to us in a continuous narrative contained in one chapter. But on closer look the narration can be broken into four connecting episodes which begin with David seeking provisions for his men (25:2-13) and end with David taking Abigail as one of his wives (25:40-43). The second episode, which is the longest and the high point of the story, tells of Abigail's meeting with David and how she prevents him from doing violence to her family and people (25:14-35). The third episode tells us of Nabal's feast and how his evil was punished (25:36-39).

First Episode: David Seeks Provisions from Nabal (25:2-11)

As in the preceding chapter, the episode happens in the same south Judean area where the desert of Maon is located. It is the time of the sheep-shearing festival, a period of traditional hospitality.[9] The event that unfolds will give us an idea of how David provided for his men in the desert. But before proceeding with the story, the narrator introduces us to the major characters: Nabal, a rich man from the mountain of Carmel who is a possible source of provision for David and his army; and Abigail, Nabal's wife. Then the narrator describes them in the following manner to give us an indication as to how the story will develop: Nabal is rough and ill-mannered, while Abigail is intelligent and beautiful (25:3).

Upon hearing of Nabal's feast, David sends ten of his men to him with a message requesting a contribution of food for his men. David's request is artfully and diplomatically done. First, he sends polite greetings ("Peace be with all that is yours"—v. 6), after which he refers to the feast and hints at Nabal's probable indebtedness ("I hear that you have shearers wth you. Now when your shepherds were with us, we did not harm them; neither did they miss anything while they were in Carmel."—v. 7). Then he finally requests to have a share in the food while maintaining a humble posture in referring to himself as "son" to Nabal ("please give them and your son David whatever you can."—25:8b).

Nabal replies brusquely. First, he tries to make David a nonentity and then equates him with a runaway servant (25:10).[10] Nabal summarily dismisses David as an unknown in spite of the respect David accorded him. Nevertheless the admirably polite language of David's message (25:6-8) does not disguise the fact that he and his men have been making a living from what amounts to a protection racket.[11] But the author does not seem to make an issue out of this. Instead he impresses upon us that the wrongdoing lies primarily in Nabal for his failure to recognize what is in his best interest even though David, strictly speaking, may not have a right to a share in the feast.[12]

The suspense heightens when the young men return to David and report Nabal's repulsive response. Seething in silent anger, David organizes punitive action against Nabal. The author ends this episode by repeating the girding of David and his men three times. In doing so, the action in effect is delayed to heighten our suspense and show us the grim determination of David and his hungry men.[13]

Second Episode: Abigail Meets with David (25:14-35)

The narrator takes us back to Nabal's farm to give us an idea of how violence will be prevented through the intervention of Nabal's intelligent wife, Abigail. There one of Nabal's servants informs Abigail of what has transpired between her husband and David's messengers. The servants further attest to the good David and his army have done them (25:14-17). Their openness with Abigail in informing her of everything that happened, including their disapproval of Nabal's actions, is indicative of how they regard her and the kind of person she is in contrast to her husband, whose boorishness is well known. Nabal's servants hold Abigail in high esteem and respect her wisdom. To them, she alone can come up with a solution to the present dilemma and avert the threatened destruction of her household ("Now think over what you should do; for our master and his entire family are surely doomed to die, but he is so wicked no one can speak to him."—25:17).

Unlike her husband, Abigail seems to know where their best interests lie.[14] She is not only quick-witted but also action-minded. She wastes no time meeting the dilemma head-on. In full command of herself, she hurries off with abundant provisions as a "peace offering" to David. She meets David just in time to deflect his seething anger. She does all this unusual action without her husband's knowledge, relying only on her intuitive wisdom and her servants' cooperation.

David and his men, in the meantime, were on their way up the mountain of Carmel when Abigail was coming down with her gifts. At this point, the narrator tells us what David was reflecting on. Still angry and nursing a hurt ego, he can think only of avenging himself for the insult he has suffered from Nabal (25:21-22). To appreciate more fully Abigail's move to avert David's vengeance, let us look at how the Old Testament people viewed this human reaction.

In Old Testament times, to avenge oneself was to punish an offense by returning evil for evil. However, in biblical language, vengeance primarily meant a reestablishing of justice, a victory over evil.[15] It was always forbidden to avenge oneself through hate for an offender, but it was a duty to avenge a violated right. But in the course of biblical history, God alone became the legitimate avenger of justice.[16] Paradoxically, as we have seen earlier, David does not have a right to the feast, therefore there was no violation of his right. If he gives in to his emotions and goes ahead with his intention to return evil for evil, he will contradict Israel's law that only God is the legitimate avenger of justice.

Perhaps Abigail had an intuition that David would take a violent course, knowing the volatile tendencies of Jewish men. This possibility is based on Israel's historical background. In early times, the members of the nomadic clan had to supply mutual protection and defense.[17] But in time, when Israel stayed in one place, there was a great need to curb human emotions always eager to render evil for evil. With the law of Talion (Exod. 21:23-33; Lev. 24, 19; Deut. 19, 21), Israelite legislation forbade the unlimited vendetta of early times (Gen. 4:15-24).

Thus, upon seeing David and his men, Abigail dismounts from her ass and puts herself in a humble stance before David by falling at his feet. Then coolheadedly she speaks to David. Theologian Bowes describes how Abigail effectively combines her speech with action:

> In a speech as skillful as David's, she first blames Nabal
> for acting the fool and herself for not seeing David's men

when they came. Pointing out that the Lord has saved David from blood guilt (v. 26), she presents her gifts.[18]

In her speech, Abigail refers to Yahweh as the One who shall prevent David from shedding blood and avenging himself (25:26). Here the narrator projects Abigail as being knowledgeable of Israel's "law of holiness," which deals with the root of revenge. It specifies the following:

You shall not have hate for your brother in your heart . . . You shall not avenge yourself and you shall not harbor rancor against members of your own race . . . (Lev. 19:17-18).

In the previous chapter, David did not avenge himself against Saul (1 Sam. 24:4-7; 26), lest he lay a hand on Yahweh's anointed.[19] Yet this same David plots to take vengeance against Nabal and all his men.[20] Abigail's skillful speech subtly reveals to David the incongruity of his intended action as she mentions her perception that because David is fighting Yahweh's battles, there is no evil in him. Exhibiting confidence in her intuition, she adds that God will establish a lasting dynasty for him (25:28).[21]

Before ending her speech, Abigail blesses David (25:29) using two metaphors. In the first, she refers to "the bundle of the living in the case of Yahweh" as David's protection against those who make attempts on his life. In the second, "she asks the Lord to hurl the lives of David's enemies as from the hollow of a sling, recalling David's victory over Goliath with a sling" (17:40, 49).[22] She ends by asking David to remember her when her predictions come true (25:30-31).

We see Abigail acting in a nontraditional way, for it is she, not David, who begins the blessing prayer. Like a priestess, she blesses David's present and future, calling on Yahweh to protect him from evil and from the hands of his enemies (25:29-31). He, in turn, blesses her for her good judgment and for keeping him from acting unjustly.

Third Episode: Nabal's Feast and Punishment

After successfully defecting David's anger, Abigail returns to Carmel. There she finds Nabal joyful and drunk while feasting in his house. In her wisdom, she says nothing to Nabal until the following day, when he has become sober. So great is Nabal's shock that he suffers a stroke upon hearing everything that Abigail has to say. He remains paralyzed for ten days until God allows him to die.

Thus, in three short verses, Nabal's life comes to an end. In simple terms, the narrator shows us through David's comments the prevailing belief at that time which was based on the theology of "divine retribution." His reaction is characteristic of Old Testament mentality wherein death is a sign of God's punishment of an evil person. The narrator says that:

> When David heard that Nabal was dead, he said, "Blessed be Yahweh who has avenged the insult I received at the hand of Nabal and has prevented me from doing wrong. Yahweh . . . has made Nabal's wrongdoings fall on his own head" (25:39).

The good David did in protecting Nabal's sheep and servants in the desert (25:15,21) is finally rewarded (25:30), while the evil Nabal showed David (25:17,21,26,39) is punished.

Fourth Episode: Abigail Becomes David's Wife (25:40-43)

This is the final episode of the story of David's encounter with Abigail. Evidently impressed not only with Abigail's beauty and wisdom but also with her generous sagacity, David wastes no time proposing marriage to her upon learning of Nabal's death. She is now the petitioned, not the petitioner. As was customary among rich and influential people in his time, he does not propose in person. Instead he sends his servants to Carmel to do the proposing.[23] Abigail, on her part, accepts David's proposal with humility ("May I be a slave to wash the feet of my lord's servants."). She has consistently taken the stance of a servant while predicting David's kingship (25:25,41). This response may not sit well with our present egalitarian view of women and men, but for a woman of her time, Abigail's response was consistent with her perception and understanding of a woman's place in ancient society. Certainly she must have considered it a great privilege to be married to Israel's future leader, even if she might be only one of his wives.[24]

David, in marrying Abigail, received not only a woman of wisdom and beauty, but most likely also control of Nabal's estate in the Calebite territory of Hebron (Josh. 14:13-14).[25] She must have been the kind of wife David needed to temper his emotions, to help him learn patience and forbearance, and to inspire confidence in him. In the narration, Abigail's marriage to David serves to introduce the mention of his marriage to Ahinoam, mother of Amnon (2 Sam. 3:2).

After this final episode, Abigail is mentioned again twice. The first is when she is taken captive by Amelekites raiding near Ziklag, but rescued along with David's other wife, Ahinoam of Jezreel (1 Sam. 30:18). The second is when she bears David a son, Chileab, at Hebron (2 Sam. 3:3). She shared David's life at Gath.

We might wonder what kind of life she lived with David and with Ahinoam, and later when David married other women. It seems as if she got lost in the shuffle. No detail is provided us. We can be certain only that she was continually exposed to danger from the enmity of Saul and from the attacks of neighboring nations. Her captivity by the Amelekites points to the greater probability that her life with David was marked by uncertainty and insecurity. It was probably a life where she was more of a widow than a queen, David having been frequently away fighting Yahweh's wars. Nonetheless it would not be unreasonable for us to conclude that she remained the wise and confident person that she was. What we saw earlier in her would be characteristic of her person for the rest of her life.

IMAGES OF FAITH AND SPIRITUALITY

Abigail's story is one of the few instances in the Bible where women are projected in an unusually nontraditional way. She is

presented more as a wise manager, a skillful speaker and nego-
tiator, and an effective decision maker who could act on her
decisions with great confidence and independence. In the area
of spirituality, the primary image of faith that Abigail is presenting to us is that of a faithful pacifist, an advocate of active
nonviolence and peace. She offers us an alternative value system, another set of ideals, another approach to leadership that
relies more on the power of peace and reconciliation than on
the power of hate and vengeance. She thus challenges us to
emotional and spiritual maturity in our responses to life.

Based on Abigail's words and actions, we can begin to draw
a portrait of a true pacifist. She or he is one who advocates
peaceful means, not war or violence, to achieve justice and reconciliation. She or he actively pursues the truth of a situation
and proclaims it not only on the personal level but also on the
interpersonal and societal levels. A pacifist is one who knows
the dangers of unchecked power and how it must be directed to
promote peace rather than war. When Nabal's servants presented Abigail with a highly volatile situation caused by Nabal's
foolish denial of David's request, she did not panic and resort
to protecting themselves from David's possible attack through
the use of force and weapons of war. Instead she chose to
address the root cause of the dilemma: David's hunger and need
for food and his rebuffed ego. Abigail thought not only of her
own good and personal safety but of the good of all, including
David and her men and even her foolish husband. She averted
a possible bloodbath by appealing to David's sense of dignity
and honor as God's anointed, thus preserving peace between
David and her people and peace in her land.

However, she could not have done what she did had she not
had faith and confidence in Yahweh's justice and goodness.
Being an intelligent woman, she must have used her mind to
understand the essence of God's law, which is for life and truth,
not death and falsehood. Being a woman of faith, she must have
prayed a lot and continually sought divine guidance for all her
actions. Her speech before David gives evidence of her wisdom
and prayerfulness. It reads as a theological reflection of her faith
in God and of her belief in pacifism. In it she skillfully follows
the principle of effective dialogue and negotiation, the highest

weapon in pursuing nonviolent action. This involves preparation and gathering of data in order to arrive at the truth of the situation; consideration of time and place of the negotiation; and knowledge of both the good and the weak points of the adversary. We see Abigail intuitively following this approach. Before she engaged in action, she listened to the information given her by her servants (1 Sam. 25:14-17), made the necessary preparations to meet David's needs (1 Sam. 25:18-19), did not waste time to meet David (1 Sam. 25:20), and relied on her intuition and knowledge regarding David's good as well as weak points as evidenced in her speech. In her dialogue with David, we find the principles of active nonviolence (ANV).

On closer examination, we see the following principles of ANV dialogue present. The *first* is to discover the truth in the other by pointing out the good she or he has done. Abigail emphasizes to David that since he is fighting the battles of Yahweh, no evil shall be found in him as long as he lives (25:28). The *second principle* is to acclaim how one has betrayed the adversary's truth and goodness. Abigail does this as she adopts a subservient position and takes the blame for everything, for not seeing the young men David had sent to her husband, and asks pardon for these. She also admits the evil disposition of her husband and implies how he has betrayed the goodness of David, who guarded Nabal's shepherds and flock in the desert (25:24-25). The *third principle* is to present the truth that one sees and how the injustice could affect both victim and adversary. She points out to David the evil effect of his intended action and proclaims her faith that for as long as David is a man of God, Yahweh will prevent him from shedding blood unjustly (25:26). The *fourth and last principle* is to propose concrete steps in which the adversary is invited to participate in coming up with an alternative solution to the dilemma. We see this concretely when Abigail makes her "peace offering" to David. Upon his acceptance of the gift, David admits seeing Abigail's point and desists from doing the unjust action. He in turn praises God for having sent Abigail to him to save him from doing evil to others (25:27, 32). The whole dialogue ends with an affirmation of Yahweh's justice and goodness through the exchange of blessings between Abigail and David. Thus, Abigail has exhibited to us the depth of her commitment to pacifism, which flows from her faith in God. Faith has given her wisdom and discernment to guide all her actions.

TODAY'S ABIGAIL

The image of Abigail in our world today may not be easily recognizable. But her presence is becoming increasingly perceptible as women grow in their consciousness of their self-worth and as they learn to claim their rights as equal partners with men in charting humanity's path toward peace, justice, and development.

We see Abigail's image in the uneducated urban poor women in third-world countries who eagerly attend literacy programs so that they may develop as persons who may no longer be manipulated in their choices of leaders in a democratic electoral process. We see her in the emancipated women who have learned to assert themselves in their homes and work places and in the political arena. We see her in the members of cause-oriented groups working to make the world a more peaceful and safe place to live. We see her in the Latin American mothers and wives of *desaparecidos* who have banded together against the powerful military in pressing for justice through peaceful means.

There she is in the active nonviolent base groups formed among laborers, farmers, fisherfolk, and urban poor dwellers. She is ever present in those who work against injustice, oppression, and other forms of violence. She is in those who try to settle disputes through peaceful means. She is also in the groups that organize themselves to push for the protection of life and of the planet Earth. She is present in women's groups that try to achieve peace through education by raising the literacy level of the poor.

Thus, whenever and wherever the spirit of nonviolence and efforts for peace and development abound, we are reminded of Abigail and all those who have followed the path of pacifism. This is the spirit we sense in the admirable work done by a team of women conducting basic education seminars for women in many localities in southern Mindanao in the Philippines.[26] The team, according to the report, is confronted with the task of arousing the interest of women in the seemingly unfamiliar topic of women's rights, and of expanding their horizons beyond housekeeping and child-rearing. For instance, the sessions conducted for women farmers include issues that touch the economic level of their lives. They discuss problems connected with the low selling prices of their produce, the adverse effects of the use of expensive insecticides on their finances and on the ecology, and other related issues along with their double burden of farming and housekeeping. The team members have evidently been challenged to devise new strategies of raising women's consciousness to empower them toward changing their marginalized condition.

Abigail's image is also reflected in the story of Nena, a young married woman and mother of two young children who lives in a poor section of Manila. For two years Nena worked in a garment factory and was the sole breadwinner for her family because Ruben, her husband, had no stable job. Her younger sister, Tita, who was living with them, babysat for her children while she was at work. Nena was contented with her situation when the labor union of which she was a member went on strike to seek higher wages and better working conditions. During the union's long strike, she had the opportunity to undergo a seminar on active nonviolence that AKKAPKA (an acronym for a peace and justice movement), a local ANV organization, offered to the striking workers. The sessions were conducted at the pickets. The team that conducted the seminar was impressed with Nena and saw in her a great potential to be a trainer in active nonviolence. She accepted AKKAPKA's offer to be a permanent staff of the ANV organization. Little did she know that the ANV formation and faith inspiration she received to follow the ANV life would prepare her to meet a serious crisis within her own family.

When Nena was out of the house with her two children, her unemployed husband came home drunk one afternoon and raped sixteen-year-old Tita, who had been left alone in the house taking a nap. Tita later related that she was startled from her nap when her brother-in-law began to rape her. She could not shout for help for he easily overpowered and restrained her.

He then threatened to kill her if she attempted to tell anybody, especially her sister, about the incident. Tita thought of running away several times, but she did not know where to go. Meanwhile Nena began to notice that Tita was becoming increasingly depressed and, as the weeks and months went by, her pregnancy became more obvious. When they were alone in the house, Nena confronted her sister about her condition. No longer able to keep everything to herself, Tita tearfully told Nena the painful truth about what happened, about the threat on her life from Nena's husband, and about her fears that she might not be believed. The sisters cried on each other's shoulders out of grief, pain, and anger.

With the truth out, Nena had to think fast. How was she going to deal with the situation and with her husband? With the help of her ANV friends, she arranged to have Tita stay in an undisclosed place indefinitely until she could confront her husband. Her friends also offered to take in her two children temporarily. Nena prayed hard while waiting for the right moment when her husband would come home sober. She knew he was basically a good person, but the series of frustrations he had encountered, especially his joblessness, had turned him into an uncaring and ill-tempered man. It hurt her to know that he could do so much physical, psychological, and spiritual damage to her sister and to their marital relationship. She also felt guilty about leaving Tita alone in the house the day of the tragedy. Nevertheless Nena tried to face all these emotions within her as she prepared to face her husband.

When the right moment came, she calmly but firmly talked to him, applying the principles of effective dialogue that she had learned in her ANV formation. Initially her husband angrily denied having anything to do with Tita's pregnancy and hastily left without letting Nena know where he was going. Nena felt she had failed in her attempt to settle the problem with him. Fearful of what he might do, she prayed and entrusted everything to God, knowing she had done the best she could under the circumstances. In the meantime an ANV friend offered to take Tita in until she gave birth. Also with the support of her ANV group, Nena was able to work out her pain and guilt.

Her husband seemed to have disappeared without a trace.

She asked his friends and relatives, but he was nowhere to be found. His disappearance added to her anguish and anxiety. A month later, he showed up at their house drunk. At first she was fearful of him, having seen in the past how easily he became violent when drunk. Spontaneously she recalled a passage from the Bible that she had meditated on in her ANV training. The line she remembered was, "If your enemy is hungry, feed him; if he is thirsty, give him something to drink; conquer evil with good." Although tempted to show her anger, as she had done in the past, she kept on praying that she would keep her cool and decided to apply what she had learned. Asking her husband if he had had anything to eat, she offered him the food she had reserved for the following day. In his drunken stupor, he sat quietly for a while, then began to devour the food as if he had never seen the likes of it in his lifetime. Nena admitted not knowing what to do nor what to feel as she watched her husband. After the meal, he leaned over the table and began to sob like a baby while mumbling to Nena that he had failed her. She felt anger and pity at the same time, yet she also thought that this was perhaps all the courage he could muster to say how sorry he was. She was relieved, at the same time realizing it was not that easy to forgive him nor to trust him again. But she felt she had to try.

After this initial reconciliation there were still many struggles and conflicts. For one thing, Nena feels that she has grown as a person while her husband has not, resulting in a huge chasm that seems to divide them emotionally and spiritually. She has tried to bridge the gap by encouraging her husband to attend the basic ANV seminar, but he always gives excuses. Far from feeling discouraged, Nena is convinced that the ANV way of life has given her inner strength and a deeper faith in God.

Nena's story, though tragic in some ways, shows us that there are many admirable people today who continue to embrace the spirit of nonviolence in spite of the violence that confronts them in their personal lives. Abigail, Nena, and all those who advocate nonviolence are witnessing to us that the way of pacifism is a more creative and godly alternative to achieve peace, reconciliation, and development.

PRAYING WITH ABIGAIL

Suggestions for Prayer and Reflection

• Read and re-read Abigail's story in the light of contemporary issues and images.

• Then reflect on the following questions: Do I see any connection between Abigail's story and the lives of those who advocate active nonviolence in our world today? What are my feelings, thoughts, and inner movements?

(Pause for reflection)

• Recall an experience of violence or injustice. What were your reactions then? How did you deal with your own tendency to conquer evil with evil?

(Pause for reflection)

• *Prayer for Peace.* Aware of the human tendency to avenge oneself (actively or passively) for hurts and injustices suffered, pray the "Prayer of St. Francis," making his words your own:

> Lord, make me a channel of your peace.
> Where there is hatred, let me bring your love.
> Where there is injury, your pardon, Lord.
> And where there is doubt, true faith in You.
>
> Lord, make me a channel of your peace.
> Where there's despair in life, let me bring hope.
> Where there is darkness, only light.
> And where there's sadness, ever joy.
>
> Oh Master, grant that I may never seek
> so much to be consoled as to console.
> To be understood as to understand,
> To be loved, as to love with all my soul.

Make me a channel of your peace.
It is in pardoning that we are pardoned.
In giving to all that we receive;
and in dying that we are born to eternal life. Amen.

Or meditate on the following passage from Paul's Letter to the Romans (12:9,14-21):

Let love be sincere. Hate what is evil and hold to whatever is good ... Bless those who persecute you; bless and do not wish evil on anyone. Rejoice with those who are joyful, and weep with those who weep. Live in peace with one another. Do not seek honors, but accept humble duties. Do not hold yourselves as wise. Do not return evil for evil, but try to earn the appreciation of others. Do your best to live in peace with everybody. Beloved, do not avenge yourselves, but let God be the one who punishes, as Scripture says: "Vengeance is mine, I will repay, says the Lord." And it adds: If your enemy is hungry, feed him; if he is thirsty, give him to drink; by doing this you will heap burning coals upon his head. Do not let evil defeat you, but conquer evil with goodness.

• *Prayer in Action.* Concretize your prayer by engaging in some action that would promote peace, reconciliation, and growth. Here are some suggestions:

— Join a local chapter of Pax Christi, a peace movement, or any cause-oriented group that advocates peaceful means in achieving its goals.
— Practice the following principles of Active Nonviolence as a way of life:
    — Always discover and proclaim the truth of the situation.
    — Protest any kind of injustice.
    — Part from injustice yourself.
    — Penetrate the conscience of the other.
    — Be prepared to pay the price or consequence.
    — Pray ceaselessly.

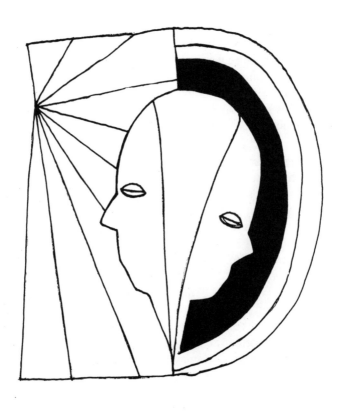

6

THE FAITH OF TWO
UNNAMED WOMEN

Women played significant roles during the period of Israel's monarchies. The stories of some of them have been incorporated in the two books of Kings. For many who are less familiar with these books, the figure of Jezebel, who outdid her husband, King Ahab, in idolatry and evil machinations, is more easily recalled than the other women characters. Yet there are other notable female figures who have significantly affected the course of Israel's history or contributed to the faith of God's people. In David's monarchy, there were Abigail and Bathsheba, and in Solomon's reign, there was the queen of Sheba.[1] There were also lesser known characters who belonged to the marginalized sector but who witnessed nonetheless to their faith in Israel's God. Such were the widow of Zarephath, a foreigner, who gave her last meal to Elijah the prophet, and the widow for whom Elisha multiplied oil.

These insignificant people were not lost in the memory of Jesus, who once said in the Gospel of Luke that "there were

133

many widows in Israel in the days of Elijah, when the heavens withheld rain for three years and six months and a great famine came over the whole land. Yet Elijah was not sent to any of them, but to a widow of Zarephath, in the country of Sidon" (Luke 4:25-26). Jesus was well aware of the untold sufferings of the poor, especially during the Deuteronomistic period of Israel's history when war was endemic. One of the roles of the prophets at that time was to mediate God's compassion and care for the poor. Through signs and wonders that sometimes accompanied their prophetic word, they announced God's displeasure with evil and God's will for the people.

At the time of the prophets Elijah and Elisha, the unusually high proportion of widows was a direct consequence of the many wars and battles fought between Israel and its neighbors. Many women lost not only their husbands but their sons as well. These widows were consigned to lives of insecurity and destitution. It was they who suffered the most when famine and other calamities struck the land. We read narratives and anecdotes about how God sent the prophets Elijah and Elisha to them to alleviate their suffering and to affirm their faith.

In the first and second books of Kings, which contain narratives of wars between Israel and Damascus, is a large grouping of stories about these great prophets. Both of them are depicted as workers of miracles whose kindness is evinced at the sight of the suffering poor, especially widows and foreigners. In this chapter we shall look at the stories of two widows: the widow of Zarephath in the First Book of Kings, and the widow whose oil was multiplied, an anecdote which appears early within the story of Elisha in the Second Book of Kings. In both stories two motifs are presented to us: the miracle of an unfailing supply of provision and God's help to those in need through the prophets' mediation.

THE WOMEN'S STORIES IN THE BIBLE

The Widow of Zarephath (1 Kings 17:7-15)

As prelude to this story, we read of how the prophet Elijah had prophesied to King Ahab that a great drought would strike

Israel because of Yahweh's displeasure over the latter's sins of idolatry and his marriage to the evil Jezebel. The drought harmed everybody, including Elijah who, to begin with, had asked God for this sign.

> [7] After a while, the brook dried up because no rain had fallen in the land. [8] Then Yahweh spoke to Elijah, [9] "Go to Zarephath of the Sidonites and stay there. I have given word to a widow there to give you food." [10] So Elijah went to Zarephath. On reaching the gate of the town, he saw a widow gathering sticks. He called to her and said, "Bring me a little water in a vessel that I may drink."
>
> [11] As she was going to bring it, he called after her and said, "Bring me also a piece of bread." [12] But she answered, "As Yahweh your God lives, I have no bread left but only a handful of flour in a jar and a little oil in a jug. I am just now gathering some sticks so that I may go in and prepare something for myself and my son to eat—and die."
>
> [13] Elijah then said to her, "Do not be afraid. Go and do as you have said, but first make me a little cake of it and bring it to me; then make some for yourself and your son. [14] For this is the word of Yahweh, the God of Israel, "The jar of meal shall not be emptied nor shall the jug of oil fail until the day when Yahweh sends rain to the earth."
>
> [15] So she went and did as Elijah told her; and she had food for herself, Elijah and her son from that day on. [16] The jar of flour was not emptied nor did the jug of oil fail in accordance with what Yahweh said through Elijah.

The Widow Whose Provision of Oil Was Multiplied (2 Kings 4:1-7)

In the fourth chapter of the Second Book of Kings, four incidents depicting the prophet Elisha as a worker of miracles are reported. The first, third, and fourth are short anecdotes, while the second, which constitutes the main body of the chapter, is a narrative.[2] However, our main concern is with the first anecdote, which constitutes the first miracle. It is about the widow whose provision of oil was multiplied. Here's the way it is narrated to us in the Bible:

[1] The widow of one of the fellow prophets called Elisha saying, "You know that my husband feared God. But now his creditor has come to collect the payment. And as we could not pay, he wanted to take my two sons as slaves." [2] Elisha said, "What can I do for you? Tell me what you have in your house?" She answered, "I have but a little oil for cleaning." [3] Elisha said to her, "Go and ask your neighbors for empty jars. [4] Get as much as you can; then go into your house with your sons and close the door. Pour oil into the vessels. And as they are filled, set them aside."

[5] The woman went and locked herself in her house with her sons. They handed her the vessels and she filled them all. [6] She said to one of her sons, "Bring me another vessel," and he answered, "There is no more." Then the oil stopped flowing.

[7] As she went back to tell this to the man of God, he said to her, "Go and sell the oil to pay for your debts; you and your sons can live on the money that is left."

A RE-READING OF THE WOMEN'S STORIES

Since the two anecdotes we shall be re-reading involve miracles, it might be beneficial to our discussion if we first examine the meaning and concept of the word miracle. Modern theology describes a miracle as "a phenomenon in nature which transcends the capacity of natural causes to such a degree that it must be attributed to the direct intervention of God."[3] Such a definition presupposes a conception of "nature" as a unity and a philosophy of nature and of natural "laws."[4] However, this is not exactly the way the Old Testament people conceived of miracles. This way of conceiving nature did not exist in ancient Near East thinking, which looked upon natural phenomena as the perceptible effects of the operations of divine personal beings, often in conflict with one another.[5] Monotheistic Israel's belief was no different except that it regarded natural phenomena as the operation of a single divine personal being. The Israelites saw the apparent conflicts in nature as the effects of the conflicts between the self-will of human beings and the supreme will of

Yahweh, who punished rebellious people through the instru-
mentality of nature.[6] The Old Testament conception of nature
was that it exhibited the constant activity of Yahweh directed
by Yahweh's providence toward humankind.[7] Lest we, as modern readers, fall into the trap of projecting onto the biblical
characters' faith our modern philosophical and theological
understanding of miracles, it would be good for us to be
reminded at the outset that in both Old and New Testaments
the emphasis in the traditions falls not on the "miraculous"
character of the events but on the "wonder" of the power and
will of Yahweh to save humankind. The traditions exhibit not
so much a faith in "miracle," an unknown concept in ancient
times, but a faith in Yahweh as the God of history and of creation who bends nature to fit One's purposes in history.[8]

It is also important to note that these miracle stories were
primarily didactic and were set in a folkloric structure intended
to catch the attention of unsophisticated hearers for whom these
were originally intended.[9] The author's main purpose in including them was to portray in a vivid way the truth that God who
gives authority to the prophets was powerfully at work in their
word.[10]

Mindful of the differences between the modern and ancient
conceptions of miracles, let us now re-read the two anecdotes
and discuss the biblical characters' faith in God's providential
care for them.

The Widow of Zarephath

In contrast to the evil and malicious Jezebel, who had threatened to have the prophet Elijah slain, was a poor and kind
woman who opened her humble home to him. She was known
only by the name of the town in which she lived—Zarephath in
Phoenicia, eight miles south of Sidon on the road to Tyre.

Alone, Elijah had been facing the apostasy of the people led
by King Ahab and his wife, Jezebel. He had prophesied that
drought would hit the land as a consequence of their sins. But
it harmed everybody, rich and poor alike, including Elijah, who
was the one who had asked God for this sign against Israel's
monarchs.

As Elijah continued to flee from Ahab and Jezebel, divine word directed him to go from Cherith to Zarephath. As Cherith to the east of the Jordan was out of Ahab's jurisdiction, so also was Zarephath, near the coast of Sidon. Outside Ahab's territory, the prophet was safe from Jezebel's wrath. He could have starved at Cherith, but God had supplied his every need, even in the midst of drought. He had drunk at the brook, and a raven had brought him bread in the morning and meat in the evening (17:6). By divine direction Elijah had come to this poor woman from Zarephath. Because Elijah's own faith had been tested and because he had learned to believe so firmly in the sustaining power of God who simply said to him, "I have given word to a widow there to give you food" (17:9), he was able to approach the humble woman of Zarephath with the positive assurance that God could supply his every need.

As he reached Zarephath's gate, he saw a widow gathering sticks. Perhaps from the widow's appearance, every indication pointed to a paradoxical situation, setting the stage for the extraordinary — the prophet being directed to a poor widow from whom help could not be expected. Elijah's double request to the woman serves to highlight the hopelessness of the situation in order to prepare the way for the miraculous:

"Bring me a little water in a vessel that I may drink." As she was going to bring it, he called after her and said, "Bring me also a piece of bread" (17:10b-11).

At first reading, one could easily react to the prophet's seemingly overbearing and demanding attitude toward a poor woman who was probably looking impoverished and emaciated. One author once commented that Elijah "asked for hospitality from a widow the way most men would order a pizza by phone."[11] The prophet sounded so insensitive to the widow's impoverished appearance as he asked for "a little water" in a time of severe drought, and for "a piece of bread" from a widow who was struggling to feed herself and her son.[12]

Aware of her social status as she stood before a person of great authority, the widow responded with characteristic humility. This was evident in her response to the prophet's first request (for a little water). She seemed to have immediately complied (11a: "As she was going to bring it . . . "). Even if the person making demands on her was a stranger, perhaps she could tell from Elijah's bearing and appearance that he was not only a prophet (because of the mantle he was wearing) but also an Israelite (because of his accent and appearance).[13] But why should he, an Israelite, come to her, a Sidonian and a heathen? Why should an Israelite prophet bother with her, a poor widow? Weren't there other people he could approach? It would be understandable for her to have some apprehensions and doubts. After all, Israel's tendency to discriminate against its pagan neighbors was legendary. Whatever questions and bewilderment she might have experienced were probably silenced when the prophet began to speak to her. His requests demanded an immediate response. The only reply she could give was an honest revelation of her hopeless situation:

> "As Yahweh your God lives, I have no bread left but only a handful of flour in a jar and a little oil in a jug. I am just now gathering some sticks so that I may go in and prepare something for myself and my son to eat—and die" (17:12).

The meaning of the woman's response to Elijah is clear: she did not have what he had asked for. Whatever was left in her possession was enough only for her and her son's last meal, after which they were prepared to perish in hunger. No doubt she was low in spirit; the radiance had gone from her face and the quickness from her step. However, despite her fatalism she must have felt that this prophet standing before her could do something—perhaps a miracle—for prophets were known to have done wondrous things in the name of their God. She therefore responded in the name and power of Elijah's God: "As Yahweh your God lives."

Though she was greatly dejected by her situation, there was a tenuous faith in her statement. Touched by her situation and her willingness to believe in Israel's God, Elijah responded to her with a message of faith and hope:

> "Do not be afraid. Go and do as you have said, but first make me a little cake of it and bring it to me; then make some for yourself and your son" (17:13).

What a test of self-renunciation for a hungry mother who was probably more conscious of her son's hunger than of her own. What a test of her faith, a faith in a God she did not even know but had heard of only from others' accounts! For someone in the depth of poverty, she had nothing more to lose by believing in the prophet's word.

She yielded to Elijah's word that he himself should be fed first from her scanty store. She made a cake as he had requested, using the flour in the barrel, mixing it with the oil in the cruse and with some water, and then frying it in oil.[14] In return for her obedience to the prophet's command, she was to know the fulfillment of the prophet's promise uttered in the name of God.

From the beginning of this incident, the theme of "word" revealed that the prophet did indeed speak a divine word, and that obedience to him would win Yahweh's favor. Yet the prophet was also subject to the word he proclaimed, which was his inner driving force although not his secure personal possession.[15] The woman's obedience to him and the word he proclaimed, in turn, had strengthened him in his own faith and vocation as a prophet. Through the faith of both woman and prophet, neither the barrel of flour nor the cruse of oil would be exhausted before the drought ended. There would be enough supply for a full year for herself, her son, and the prophet.

Even in the midst of drought, the widow of Zarephath was to experience the continual miracle of nature in all its abundance. Moreover, she would be in the center of this miracle because she had been willing to give all she had and because she was willing to believe in Elijah's God, even if she had no knowledge of who this God was.

Thus from start to finish the short anecdote has not failed to provide us with contrasts and paradoxes. We have seen how Ahab's sins brought suffering to the people of Israel, while Elijah's fidelity to God brought nourishment to the poor. Two non-Israelite women—Queen Jezebel and the nameless widow—played contrasting roles in the prophet's life. One, wicked and powerful, drove him into exile and homelessness, while the other, humble and powerless, opened her home to him. Jezebel's hatred for Elijah was murderous, while the widow's hospitality and generosity were life-giving. A rich queen would go down to her death fighting God, while a poor widow would come back to health and plenty because she believed in God.

A parallel story to this miraculous provision of food is the prophet Elisha's multiplication of a widow's oil. This second incident happened many years later and is simply recounted to us as one of the series of anecdotes about Elisha's prophetic activities. Let us now re-read it in the light of our understanding of the Old Testament prophetic traditions.

The Widow Whose Provision of Oil Was Multiplied

The story of this second widow could easily be lost in the rapid succession of events in the prophet Elisha's life. This first miracle is followed by several others which, if not more important, were more wondrous in the eyes of many, like the raising to life of the Shunammite's son (2 Kings 4:8-37) and the healing of Naaman's leprosy (2 Kings 5:1-27).

Like the widow of Zarephath, this second widow is unnamed. All we know about her is that her husband was a prophet. So insignificant was her identity that the writer did not even bother to mention the place from which she came. We can only guess that the incident happened in Carmel, as verse 25 locates Elisha in that place.[16]

The widow had no claim to the compassion of the prophet, except that he had known her husband, who "did fear the Lord" (4:1a). Her husband had died, leaving debts so heavy that his creditors came and demanded that as payment her two sons be given them to be slaves (4:1b).[17] Evidently her husband left no property, so she seemed to have no alternative but to give up her sons to slavery. She was understandably distressed, for she was well aware of Hebrew law, which allowed the selling of wife and children into slavery to settle a debt (Exod. 21:7). Compared to the Hammurabi Code which provided the release of those sold into slavery after three years,[18] Hebrew law was much stiffer. It permitted Hebrew slaves freedom only after six years of service (Exod. 21:2) although they could be released earlier if the Jubilee year, which was celebrated every fifty years, fell within their six-year service (Lev. 25:39-55). For this poor mother, the creditors' demand would mean a life of greater destitution for her and the virtual loss of her two sons, whom she might never see again, considering her age and situation.

It was in this situation of great need that she humbly approached Elisha for help. Unless she could pay her husband's debts, she would have to part with her sons. She would do anything and everything to keep her family together and to save her sons from a life of slavery. Moved with pity for her and desiring to help her, Elisha responded with a double question. The first, "What can I do for you?" (4:2a), sounds as though Elijah was still groping for answers on how to help the poor widow whose dead husband he had known. Without waiting for a response to his first question, he asked the second, "Tell me what you have in your house" (4:2b). From the tone of this second question, we get a hint that the prophet already knew what to do or at least was exploring some solution in his mind, although the widow may not have perceived it yet. To this second question, the widow sadly responded, "Your maidservant has nothing in the house, except a jar of oil" (4:2c, RSV).[19]

Elisha's planned solution would involve her investment of whatever little was left in her possession, which was "a jar of oil." Little did she know that this precious oil would prove its true value. Through the prophet's faith, this small provision of oil would soon be multiplied and used to solve the widow's problem. How? And why, of all things, "oil"? To understand the wisdom behind Elisha's planned solution, let us consider the significance and symbolism of oil in biblical times.

Along with wheat and wine, oil was among the essential food with which God had filled the Chosen People in the land rich in olive trees where God gratuitously established Israel (Deut. 11:14). Its abundance was a sign of salvation (Joel 2:19) and a symbol of eschatological happiness (Hos. 2:24).[20] In ancient Palestine, as in most of the ancient world, oil, especially olive oil, was a valuable and marketable commodity because of its many uses. It was often mentioned in the list of the products of Palestine. It was an evidence of prosperity (Deut. 8:8; 14:23) and was often used as a medium of exchange before coinage was invented. For instance, Solomon paid Hiram of Tyre thousands of gallons of oil for laborers and materials furnished for the Jerusalem Temple (1 Kings 5:11).

Oil as a condiment was an important part of the ancient people's diet (Deut. 32:13; Judg. 9:9; Ezek. 16:13; Hos. 2:7). It took the place of butter in cooking. Mixed with meal, oil was used for offerings to the Deity. As a medicine, it was used in the anointing of wounds (Isa. 1:6). As a refreshing unguent (Deut. 28:40) and as the base of the mixture of perfumes such as myrrh and nard, it was used after a bath (2 Sam. 12:20; Ruth 3:3) as a sign of joy and of festive attire. It was also a ceremonial unguent used in the anointing of a person's head as a sign of divine election. It was likewise the usual fuel for the lamp, usually in connection with the lamp in the sanctuary (Exod. 27:20; Lev. 24:2).

Thus oil could easily be sold or exchanged for other goods because of its high value and usefulness. But what use would a "little oil" be to a widow whose debts were so great? Even if she were to sell it, the amount she would get would probably not be sufficient to cover her entire debt. This paradoxical situation would again pave the way for the miraculous to happen. The widow had to trust and obey the prophet, who simply instructed her on what to do.

> Elisha said to her, "Go and ask your neighbors for empty jars. Get as much as you can; then go into your house with your sons and close the door. Pour oil into the vessels. And as they are filled, set them aside" (4:3-4).

The prophet left it to the widow to expect that a multiplication of her meager provision of oil would happen. But to carry out his simple orders, she, together with her two sons, had to possess a childlike and trusting faith. The cooperation of her two sons was needed. For the miracle to happen, all three of them had to pray and work together as a family in the privacy of their humble home. And so it came to pass that all the vessels were filled, including those they had borrowed from their neighbors. It was only then that the oil stopped flowing, leaving them an abundance of the precious commodity (4:5-6).

As soon as all the containers of the entire neighborhood were filled, the widow went back to the prophet to tell him what had happened. Understandably she would want Elisha to be the first person to know about the miracle; after all, he had been instrumental in making it happen. However, her going back to the prophet could also be read differently, considering the position of women at that time. It would not be unreasonable to think that, having been dependent all her life on her husband, as expected of women during that period, she had no consciousness nor experience whatsoever as a person to exercise her human right and authority over her life and future. Neither did she have the experience of being the breadwinner for the family. These were not part of women's and men's consciousness in biblical times. Now that she was widowed, she had to learn how to make decisions for herself, especially in matters concerning her life and the future of her two sons. Her going to Elisha could mean either that she did not know what to do with the abundant supply of oil, or that it was simply out of deference to the kind prophet that she did not do anything without first consulting him.

Whatever interpretation of her actions we might prefer, the conclusion is quite clear: the woman from then on had to be involved in business, using as capital the abundant supply of precious oil in her possession to generate income for herself and her family. The supply was enough to give the poor widow lifelong security. Elisha had provided for her future, had taught her an independent way of providing for her family as a single parent, and had given her the added blessing of keeping her sons by her side.

IMAGES OF FAITH AND SPIRITUALITY

The separate anecdotes of the two women who experienced God's providence through the multiplication of their meager resources speak to us of the "miracle" that can happen in our midst when we believe in God's providential care and power and when we learn to use and share our gifts and resources with others.

The faith of these two women was very simple. In the story of the widow of Zarephath, this poor woman on the fringes of society—a widow in the world of the married and a Gentile dealing with an Israelite prophet — gave everything she had in a supreme moment of faith, hope, and charity, and her generosity was greatly rewarded, "as Yahweh had foretold through Elijah."[21] In the story of the widow whose provision of oil was multiplied, this poor mother oppressed by the laws and structures of society approached God through the prophet in humility and confidence that he, God's messenger, could save her sons from slavery. Because she believed in the prophet's word and obeyed his command, trusting only that he spoke in the name of Yahweh, she experienced "an abundance of oil," a sign of God's salvation and a symbol of eschatological happiness. The "oil" saved her two sons from slavery and allowed her to experience the joy of being united with her loved ones — a foretaste of eschatological happiness.

Through their miracle stories, these two women have shown us images of faith worth examining in the light of the ongoing oppression of the marginalized; the self-absorption of many in their quest for power, happiness, and fulfillment; and the faithlessness and compulsive competitiveness that characterize our technological society. Their stories remind us of the biblical faith and spiritual values which our secularized world has grossly forgotten or minimized and which we need to reclaim, namely: (1) faith in the gratuitous power of God, (2) hospitality as a primary virtue that gives witness to faith, and (3) faith that inspires unity and cooperation within the family or community, and confidence in one's own gifts, potentials, and capabilities.

Faith That Believes in God's Gratuitous Power

Although the focus of the two miracle stories was not the miracles themselves but the faith of the two women, it is also clear that the miracles were the very instruments through which God's gratuitous power was manifested. Beyond the astonishment which miracles arouse, they aim at provoking and confirming faith and its accompaniments: confidence, thanksgiving, and memory (Ps. 105:5).[22] We saw this in the attitudes and responses of the two women. They showed confidence in the prophets' words, and when the miracles happened, they manifested their thanksgiving to God not through words but through action. The

widow of Zarephath, in thanksgiving to God, provided a home
for Elijah until the drought ended, while the widow whose oil
was multiplied went back to Elisha to report the miracle and
through his further advice used her God-given potential and
capabilities to stand on her own two feet and manage the livelihood of her own family. These minor incidents were etched in
the memory of God's people and recorded for the sake of the
faith of future generations.

The attitudes and responses of the women likewise inspire
humility, obedience, "fear of God,"[23] and hope. These are vir-
tues that have become increasingly rare in a world that is bent
on dominance and control; in a society that recognizes as ultimate goals riches, power, and influence; and in human hearts
that hunger for recognition through worldly success and achievements.[24] Because they humbly obeyed God's word as spoken
through the prophets, the wonders that happened before their
very eyes instilled in their hearts greater awe or "fear of God"
and turned their sorrows into joy.

The spirit of hospitality likewise characterized the women's
faith—the widow of Zarephath by sharing her last meal and
accepting the prophet and his God, and the second widow by
opening her heart to the prophet's instructions. In their own
way and circumstance, they witnessed to faith.

Hospitality as a Witness to Faith

In a world scarred by violence, crime, and exploitation and
ruled by compulsive competition and self-absorption, security—
both personal and national—becomes an obsessive concern. The
practice of hospitality as a primary virtue in such an atmosphere
becomes a grave risk for any person or society. Hospitality
becomes a rare commodity, reserved mostly for family and
friends, not strangers and paupers. To us who hunger for meaning and real happiness, the widow of Zarephath has a basic
lesson to teach: the true virtue of hospitality!

What is the biblical meaning of this virtue? How did the
ancient people practice it? What place does it have in our Christian faith? To answer these questions, let us first trace its roots
in the Old Testament as well as its practice from the time of

the patriarchs until the New Testament period.

In ancient times hospitality was the kind and gracious reception of guests characteristic of the various peoples of the biblical world. It was tightly bound up in customs and practices that all were expected to observe. As in an intricately choreographed dance, in which any participant who does not observe his or her part must either learn it or leave the dance so as not to mess up the entire presentation, so it was with the customs of ancient hospitality.[25] It was carefully structured and rigidly observed as a process of "receiving" outsiders and changing them from strangers to guests.[26] It was therefore different from the kind of reception one normally extended to relatives and friends.

Hospitality was a feature of the seminomadic life of the patriarchal era as depicted in the Genesis narratives, which reveal customs still observed by the Bedouin tribes of today.[27] For them the entertainment of strangers was a sacred obligation, based on something more than supplying food, lodging, and fellowship for the wayfarer. Hospitality was offered with the feeling that one might be entertaining "angels unaware" (Gen. 18:2, 19:1), and that one might oneself become as dependent as the person now seeking it.[28] The Old Testament considered this hospitable attitude toward strangers a primary virtue. We recall Abraham extending hospitality to strangers who turned out to be angels in disguise (Gen. 18:1-8). He provided water for their feet and a place underneath a tree to rest. He prepared the heavy part of the feast and summoned Sarah to bake fresh "cakes upon the hearth." There are many other examples and details of how hospitality was extended during this period, such as Rebekah offering a pitcher of water from the family well to a newly arrived stranger and all his beasts. Even when Israel had settled down in towns, the proverbial hospitality persisted.

As a sacred obligation, hospitality became a way of witnessing to one's faith in Yahweh as Israel reflected on its relationship with God and grew in its knowledge of the Holy One. The hospitality the Israelites were expected to extend the stranger passing through was a reminder to Israel of its former condition as an enslaved stranger (Lev. 19:33–34). It also served to remind Israel of the present condition of a traveler upon earth (Ps. 39:13). Although there were despicable breaches in hospitality recorded in biblical history,[29] these cases did not alter significantly the people's custom and practice of hospitality.

But the urbanization of Israel and the sociopolitical transformations that accompanied the monarchy were slowly destroying the ethic of sharing characteristic of the old family-centered traditional society.[30] Divisions between rich and poor rapidly ensued. Hospitality, which was the rule of life of a pilgrim people, slowly gave way to suspicion of strangers and exploitation of the poor. At a time when Israel grew in faithlessness because of the wicked influence of its rulers and lost the practice of true hospitality, it was a starving widow from Zarephath, a foreigner and a pagan, who gave witness to a vibrant faith in Israel's God. By giving her last meal to Elijah, she demonstrated in a radical way the kind of hospitality that Israel had forgotten. Approached by a total stranger, whom she probably recognized as a prophet through the mantle he was wearing, she willingly gave all that she had even if it would mean deprivation for her and her son. Although she did not belong to Israel's faith, she accepted not only the prophet but Israel's God as well.

In the New Testament, this was the dimension of faith in the widow that Jesus himself commended when he experienced the inhospitable attitude of his own townspeople at the inauguration of his public ministry. Reacting to his people's faithless attitude toward him, he recalled the rejections experienced by the great prophets Elijah and Elisha:

> "Truly I say to you, no prophet is acceptable in his own country. But in truth, I tell you, there were many widows in Israel in the days of Elijah, when the heaven was shut up three years and six months, when there came a great famine over all the land; and Elijah was sent to none of them but only to Zarephath, in the land of Sidon, to a woman who was a widow. And there were many lepers in Israel in the time of the prophet Elisha; and none of them was cleansed, but only Naaman the Syrian" (Luke 4:24-27).

The lack of hospitality shown by God's own people was tantamount to a lack of faith. Because of their rejection of him,

God would instead open the kingdom not to them, Yahweh's Chosen People, but to others who were generous enough to welcome him unreservedly.

In Jesus' parable on the Last Judgment he also emphasized hospitality as a witness to true faith. In it he revealed to everyone the mystery of this hospitality which is a form of charity.[31] Christ himself will welcome or send away according to how he was treated as a guest, recognized or unrecognized (Matt. 25:35–46). It was not only at his birth that there was no room for him in the inn (Luke 2:7). It was right up to the end of his life that the world did not recognize him and his own did not receive him (John 1:9–13). He proclaimed that those who believe in him receive his disciples "in his name" (John 13:20) as well as the poor and the marginalized. Those who welcome "these little ones" in the spirit of hospitality truly welcome him.

Faith's Capacity To Inspire Unity, Cooperation, and Self-Confidence

Another dimension of faith that is implied in the two miracle stories is its capacity to inspire unity and cooperation within one's family or community and confidence in one's own gifts, potentials, and capabilities. This is more pronounced in the story about the widow whose provision of oil was multiplied. It was her faith in the prophet's every word that enabled the miracle to happen.

Yet more amazing than the actual miracle itself were the lessons she learned from following the prophet's instructions which transformed her from a helpless widow to an independent woman capable of providing for her own family. The prophet, instead of giving her the money she needed to pay her husband's debt like a "dole-out," taught her a more creative way of dealing with her predicament. First, he made her realize through their initial dialogue that she had something in her possession that could be used as an investment for the solution of her problem: the little oil she owned. Then from his instructions, she came to see that the problem she was carrying was as much her sons' as it was her own. She alone could not handle it. Her two sons had to be involved in working for its solution. But getting their cooperation was not enough. An essential part of the prophet's instruction that she and her two sons had to follow was "to shut the door upon herself and her sons." In biblical parlance, this means that she and her sons had to pray earnestly and in prayer find unity and cooperation among themselves to do what the prophet had instructed them. Only then did the miracle happen—there was an abundance of oil, a sign of God's saving help.

Yet what she and her sons learned by obeying the prophet's word was not enough to surmount their grave family problem. She had to become aware that the fruits of her prayer must flow into action. When she returned to the prophet to tell him of the miracle, she was further instructed to go and sell her oil and use the money to pay her husband's debts and use the rest as a source of livelihood for herself and her sons. She had to learn to trust in herself and in her capacities to stand firm in a society that considered women as dependent and helpless. Because she trusted and prayed earnestly, she and her sons experienced God's saving power. Her faith likewise enabled her to discover her own capacities and potentials as a person.

THE UNNAMED WOMEN OF TODAY

The situation of women in general and widows in particular in today's society may not be as bleak compared to that of the widows in biblical times. Just the same, many women today are often left with too many burdens to carry, especially if they are poor. In both the Old and New Testament, widows sometimes found that the guardians of the very law that supposedly protected them had turned into unscrupulous specialists preying on these poor women. We can say that the same is also true now. We often hear of uniformed law enforcers who get their regular "food allowance" from poor sidewalk vendors who do not have licenses to do their trade. Or when law enforcers round up the illegal vendors, oftentimes it is the women vendors who are apprehended because they can not run as fast as the men. The women are asked to pay heavy fines, and their goods are confiscated.

There are many more stories of untold suffering and oppression experienced by widows and single mothers today. There are many single mothers—widowed, separated, or abandoned by their husbands—who struggle to feed themselves and their children or sometimes are forced to sell their children in order to survive or give them up for adoption to assure them of a better future. Often these single mothers are the first victims of calamities, both natural and human-made, and of a country's worsening socio-economic condition. We can be certain that in the hearts of these poor women is a dream or a hope that some miracle would happen in their lives to alleviate their poverty. One widow once commented that there have been moments in her life when she wished that when she woke up in the morning things would be different. But when she would hear her children crying of hunger she would suddenly snap out of her daydream and worry again about where to get their next meal.

These are the women who, like the widow of Zarephath and the widow whose oil was multiplied, are continually awaiting God's help. While others have given up hope in their helplessness and desperation, there are those who cling to their faith, hoping that someday God will relieve them of their suffering and burdens. Like the woman whose oil was multiplied, some of these women have discovered a little resource within themselves through the help and encouragement of concerned Christians and civic-minded people.

Such is the case of the women who belong to BEMAI (Bato-Ermita Mothers Association, Inc.). This association, which started in 1986, is composed of urban poor mothers living in a squatter area in Cebu in the southern Philippines. Many of them are single mothers—widowed, separated, abandoned, or with jobless husbands. In the past, several organizations had tried to help the people in the area get started on some livelihood projects, but these were not too successful because the people did not know how to pay back their small loans.

Through the efforts of the parish priest and a religious sister working in the area, the mothers of young children were organized. Their first project was a day-care center. To become members, the mothers had to attend regular formation programs and monthly meetings and help out in the center. This was the beginning of their slow but steady success as an association. In time they were able to set up a family clinic with volunteer health workers to meet their members' health needs. Nonmembers who lived in the area could also avail themselves of the services. Through their initial efforts, the women were able to convince a local funding agency to help them in their livelihood projects. But the women have to come up with individual small projects to qualify for loans. Since they live near a market, most of them find that selling fruits, vegetables, and snacks are feasible projects. Apprehensive that the members would again renege on their obligation to pay their loans, the leaders initiated a collection system that would take into consideration the "hand-to-mouth" mentality of the poor. Under the system, a percentage of their daily earnings is collected each day as payment for their loan and as forced savings.

Encouraged by their initial success, during their monthly meetings and formation sessions, the women continue to discuss group projects that would benefit the community as a whole. One of their recent projects was to provide clean running water in the area. They were able to get the government water system to connect a water pipe in their area. They have also set up a cooperative that manages the common well where the members can buy clean water at a cheaper price. These little successes have made the women realize that if they continue to pray for God's help and at the same time cooperate with one another, they will be able to surmount their many problems. Truly God will help only those who are willing to help themselves. Prayer and action must go together. As a group, the women came to realize that they must support and encourage one another. They have been able to succeed in their small projects because they learned to believe in their God-given gifts and potentials. Their successes may seem small, but when viewed against their past, they are like giant steps toward their growth as individuals and as a community. The story of the women's group may not be a big miracle story, but it is a miracle nonetheless, and they are grateful to God that they are part of the miracle.

Therefore, as the women of old and of today have shown us, making room in our lives for the unexpected stranger or for God's mysterious plan is a special form of hospitality. When we believe in possibilities, using whatever gifts we have in our person, we also make room for happy surprises to happen and for incredible promises to be fulfilled.

PRAYING WITH THE TWO WOMEN

Suggestions for Prayer and Reflection

• Read and re-read the two miracle stories in the light of contemporary issues, situations, and images.

• Then reflect on the following questions: Do I see any connection between the widows' situations and those of today's widows and single mothers? What are my feelings and inner movements?

(Pause for reflection)

• Identify with the women's situation by recalling a personal experience of great need. What were your feelings? How did you respond in faith to your situation? Where was God in your experience? How did you experience God's saving power in the solution of your problem?

(Pause for reflection)

• *Prayer for Mercy.* Lift up to God the suffering poor of today as you say the following prayer:

> God,
> yesterday I saw
> flashed on T.V.
> the emaciated faces
> and wasted bodies
> of women and children,
> of the old and the crippled,
> starving to death
> in some distant shore.
> All victims of war,
> famine,

drought,
human neglect,
greed,
and insensitivity.

But when I look around me
in my neighborhood and city,
I see the same images.
They are not really so far away from me.
Their desperate, hopeless faces
stare me in the eye,
and hound me.
They crowd my consciousness.
They prick my conscience.
No wonder I prefer to be blind and numb,
I am afraid to be touched by their suffering
and disturbed from my security.
For here I am
well fed,
clothed,
educated,
and rich in opportunities,
but have not shared.

Forgive me,
God of the poor and the suffering.
Shake me,
disturb me,
and grant me your holy discomfort,
that I may learn
to open my heart,
my home,
and my life
to you
and to the least of your
brothers and sisters.

Remind me of what you said
long ago—

"Truly, I say to you:
whatever you did not do
for one of the least of these,
you did not do to me."
Amen.

• *Prayer in Action.* Concretize your prayer by engaging in some action that would alleviate the sufferings of the poor and the marginalized. Here are some suggestions:
—Share your food with the hungry.
—Open your home to the homeless.
—Visit a home in a poor area near you.
—Be involved with organizations that aim at empowering women in the urban or rural poor areas.

• *Other Scripture Suggestions for Prayerful Reflection:*
1. Parallel miracle stories in the New Testament:
—The hospitality of the widow of Zarephath is echoed in the story of the widow's mite. Jesus lauds the generous heart of this poor widow (Luke 21:1-4).
—The faith of the widow whose oil was multiplied foreshadows the faith of Mary in the multiplication of the wine at Cana. Both are foretastes of eschatological happiness (John 2:1-11).
2. New Testament passages on the meaning and significance of hospitality in Jesus' life and in the life of the first Christian community:
—Jesus extended hospitality to hungry multitudes (Mark 8:1-9),
—and accepted it from a ruler of the Pharisees (Luke 14:1-11);
—from the family at Bethany (Matt. 21:17; John 12:2);
—from the penitent Zacchaeus at Jericho (Luke 19:5-10);
—and from his bewildered hosts at Emmaus (Luke 24:29-31).
—The beginning of the Lord's Supper was a shared meal in a Jerusalem guest chamber, prepared under Christ's direction (Mark 14:15; Luke 22:7-13).

—The historic events of Pentecost also occurred in a large guest room in Jerusalem (Acts 2:2).
—Paul, realizing the evil atmosphere of most first century inns, urged his followers to accept private hospitality and expected Christians to extend it to traveling believers (Rom. 12:13; 1 Pet. 4:9),
—as Jesus expected it for his disciples (Matt. 10:9-15; Luke 10:4-16).

PART II

PRAYERS
BY WOMEN
OF THE
OLD TESTAMENT

7

MIRIAM

Exodus 2, 15:1 — 21; Numbers 12

The Prophetess Miriam

There are a few women who are recognized as religious leaders in the Old Testament. Miriam, the sister of Moses and Aaron, is one of them. She first appeared in the second chapter of the Book of Exodus as a small girl. Unnamed then, she was simply identified as "the sister of the child." This was the time when Egypt's pharaoh, threatened by the rising population of the Hebrews, had ordered all the Hebrew male infants slain. It is presumed that Miriam was the same sister who stood guarding Moses, her baby brother, as he lay in a basket placed among the reeds near the bank of the river Nile. When the daughter of the wicked pharaoh discovered the baby while taking a bath in the river, she took pity on the infant and decided to adopt him. That was when Miriam approached her quietly, asking if she would like her to find a Hebrew woman to nurse the baby. And so it was that the baby's mother became his own nurse in the safety of the pharaoh's palace.

When Miriam appears on the scene again, Israel's deliverance is at hand. At this time she was known as a *prophetess*, which in Hebrew means a woman inspired to teach the will of God. The word is also used for wife of a prophet and is sometimes applied to a singer of hymns.[1] Since the Bible gives no record that she was ever married, we can assume that she was known more for her inspiration to teach God's will as well as lead in singing praise and thanksgiving to God at important events in Israel's history. At the crossing of the Sea of Reeds, the central event of Israel's history, Miriam, with a tambourine in her hand, led the women in festive dance, singing to the people: "Sing to Yahweh the glorious one, horse and rider he has thrown into the sea" (15:21). The preceding song, which has the same refrain, was sung by Moses and the Israelites (Exod. 15:1), but it was Miriam who was identified as the leader of the song.[2] What her part was in the composition of this national anthem is not known, but she had an equal share with Moses and Aaron in weaving it into the conscious life of Israel.[3]

In the wilderness Miriam apparently continued to occupy a leadership role as prophetess. However, there came a point when the relationship among the three leaders — Moses, Aaron, and herself — became problematic. Miriam and Aaron were involved in a dispute with Moses, sparked by the latter's choice of a wife, but their complaint was focused more on the function of leadership in the community. Both she and Aaron challenged Moses' role as prophet. "Has Yahweh only spoken through Moses? Has he not also spoken through us?" (Num. 12:2).

God heard their complaint. Summoning the three leaders to the Tent of Meeting, God upheld Moses as the primary leader, for to him alone did the Holy One speak face to face. Although Miriam's leadership could not be denied, God punished her nonetheless for her indiscretion. She was stricken with leprosy and was healed only when Moses appealed to God on her behalf. As a modern reader, one might wonder why Aaron was spared the punishment while he too was involved in the dispute. One can only make sense out of it by considering the patriarchal context in which the account was written. Nevertheless, it is made clear that in the wilderness Moses was the undisputed leader and prophet. All other prophets, including Miriam, were also leaders, but they had to recognize that they were still responsible to the top position.[4]

Like her brothers, Miriam never entered the Promised Land. The final scene in her story was her death in Kadesh. Here her people gave her the honor that she deserved as a leader. According to tradition, after her death her funeral was celebrated in the most solemn manner for thirty days. She is forever remembered in her song of exaltation.

The Song of Miriam

The prayer in Exodus 15:21 that Miriam sang is very brief, consisting only of a single strophe of two couplets.[5] It was probably from this ancient brief song that the "Song of the Sea" (Exod. 15:1a-18) was developed, although other biblical scholars opine that this is only the title of the long one in 15:1-18.[6] This is why the song is also called the "Song of Miriam." The song itself has been given many other titles, such as the "Song of Deliverance," the "Song of Moses," the "Song of Moses and Miriam," and the "Song of the Sea." Whatever title we might prefer to give it, one thing is certain: Miriam will always be recognized as its song leader.

Here is her song:[7]

> I will sing to you Yahweh, the glorious one,
> horse and rider you have thrown into the sea.
> Yahweh, you are my strength and my song,
> and you are my salvation.
> You are my God and I will praise you;
> the God of my ancestors: I will extol you.
>
> You are a warrior: Yahweh is your name.
> The chariots of Pharaoh and his army
> you have hurled into the sea;
> his chosen officers were drowned in the Red Sea.
> The deep covers them;
> they went down like a stone.
> Your hand, O Yahweh, glorious and powerful,
> your right hand, O Yahweh, shatters the enemy.

In the splendor of your majesty you crush your foes;
you send forth your fury, which devours them like stubble.
At the blast of your nostrils the waters piled up.
the surging waters stood firm in heap;
the deeps congealed in the heart of the sea.

The enemy said, "I will give chase and overtake,
I will divide the spoil and make a feast of it.
I shall draw my sword and my hand will destroy them."
A breath of yours and the sea covered them;
they sank like lead in the mighty waters.

Who among the gods is like you, Yahweh?
Who is like you, majestic in holiness,
awesome in power, doing wonders?
You stretched out your right hand;
the earth swallowed them.

In unfailing love you guide the people you redeemed,
in strength you lead them to your holy house.
Hearing this, the nations tremble;
anguish grips the people of Philistia.
The chieftains of Edom are dismayed;
the leaders of Moab are seized with trembling;
the people of Canaan melt away.

Terror and dread fall upon them.
your powerful arm leaves them still as stone
until your people pass by, O Yahweh!
till the people you have purchased pass by.

You will bring them in and plant them
on the mountain of your inheritance,
the place you chose to dwell in, O Yahweh,

the sanctuary prepared by your hands.
Yahweh will reign forever! (Exod 15:1-18)

PRAYING WITH MIRIAM

Prayer Experience

• To let the prayer experience flow more smoothly, read the instructions ahead of time until you become more familiar with the process. Then proceed at your own pace and make your own adaptation if you wish.

• Or record the instructions on a cassette recorder, pausing whenever the three dotted marks (. . .) appear. This way you can follow your own pace during the prayer process.

• If you plan to use this with a group, have someone lead the prayer process.

1. Breath-Prayer. Be still and become aware of your own breathing . . . Close your eyes so that you can focus your attention inwardly . . . Allow the rhythm of your own breathing to quiet your whole body and inner being . . . Let your breathing sweep your mind and clear it of thoughts and distractions . . . While breathing in, say to yourself God's name, "O God," or "Yahweh". . . While doing so; become aware of God's presence entering your body and whole being as you breathe in . . . and while breathing out, repeat to yourself the words "Save me from distress." (You may choose your own mantra or phrase if you wish.) . . . As you breathe out, repeating the second part of the mantra to yourself, allow all your tensions, anxieties, and negative feelings to leave your body until slowly you feel a sense of deep relaxation. Do this for a few moments, allowing your rhythmic breathing to relax your body and to take you deeper and deeper into the center of your inner self . . . the place where you shall experience deep silence and oneness with God and yourself . . .

2. Prayer Using One's Memory or Imagination. Do either of the following prayer suggestions:

• *Memory*. Recall an experience when you were saved from a certain crisis. Become aware of your feelings while recalling such an experience. Try to enter into them again — feelings of anxiety and worry turning into feelings of relief, joy, and thanksgiving. Then read Exodus 15:1-18 slowly and prayerfully.

• *Guided Imagery*. Become quiet and take a few deep, slow breaths . . . Imagine being part of God's people as they crossed the Sea of Reeds, Pharaoh's army and chariots pursuing you. What is it like being with the people, fearful of the enemy overcoming them? . . . Then as you reach the safety of the shore, you look back together with Miriam and the rest of the people . . . You see the tide of the sea engulfing the enemies — horse and chariot are cast into the sea, with the currents swirling about them, with the breakers and the billows passing over and above them . . . Try to enter into these images of distress, recalling your own feelings when you were in such condition, when you felt like drowning in the sea of problems and demands . . . What was prayer like for you during those critical moments? . . . Stay with these images for as long as you wish . . . Allow the Spirit to take you and lead you to wherever God wishes you to go in your guided meditation . . . Then imagine yourself celebrating among the people with Miriam leading the song of thanksgiving . . . Feel the relief of each one . . . Recall your experience when your crisis was over . . . What was your prayer like at that time? . . . Stay with your feelings for a while . . . then read Exodus 15:1-18 slowly and prayerfully as your own prayer of praise and thanksgiving to God.

3. Prayer in Action. Here are some suggestions that will help you concretize your own prayer:

- Extend a helping hand to someone who is in crisis.
- Share with someone your experience of God's saving help.
- Celebrate your freedom as a child of God by appreciating your gift of life.

8

DEBORAH

Judges 4:1–5:31

Deborah: Judge, Prophet, Deliverer

At the time of the judges some thirteen centuries before Christ, there rose another female political and religious leader. Her name was Deborah. She lived in Tomer-Deborah in the hill country of Ephraim. In the Hebrew community, she occupied several leadership roles. As a prophet who spoke God's message, she was counselor to her people. As a judge, she must have settled their disputes with wisdom and spiritual insight. So great was their trust in her that she was placed at the height of political power by the common consent of the people.[1] She filled the position of judge in much the same way that Jephthah and Gideon did as Israel's administrator and military leader. This was when the Israelites were being oppressed by the Canaanites under their king, Jabin, and their military commander, Sisera. In her role as deliverer in time of war, Deborah exhibited great courage and total dependence on God who alone could deliver her and her people from their enemies.

Summoning Barak and in the name of Yahweh, she ordered him to organize an army of ten thousand men from Zebulon and Naphtali near Mt. Tabor. Barak, however, refused to go unless Deborah accompanied him. She agreed, declaring that "the Lord will deliver Sisera into the hand of a woman" (Judg. 4:9b). Even if she did not actually lead the army in battle, she made the military decisions. Unlike Miriam, who was a secondary leader responsible to the top position, Deborah was a primary leader with a man responsible to her.[2]

In the course of the battle, what she earlier prophesied came true. Sisera did fall into the hands of a woman, but they were not hers. It was another courageous woman, a Kenite by the name of Jael, who delivered the final blow to the Canaanite commander by thrusting a tent peg into his forehead with a hammer while he was asleep in her tent. Upon Sisera's death, God humbled Jabin before the Israelites. To celebrate their victory, Deborah, together with Barak, sang a prayer of praise and thanksgiving to Yahweh.

The Song of Deborah

The prayer, set in poetic form, is known as the "Song of Deborah." It is one of the oldest examples of biblical literature, dated around 1125 B.C.E. and roughly contemporaneous with the events it describes.[3] It combines two great themes — Yahweh's control over all of creation and Israel's unity as a nation of tribes. However, it is not clear whether Deborah is the speaker of the poem or the person to whom it is spoken.[4] It is plain that a battle is narrated in which Yahweh defeats Israel's opponent by making it rain.[5] It has a repetitive style like older Canaanite poetry from Ugarit.[6] It graphically portrays the excitement of the battle in which God is recognized as the real leader of the Israelite army. It also describes the cosmic forces joining Israel in their battle against the enemy. The middle portion describes the brave participation of some of Israel's tribes and the lack of response of the others. The final portion of the poem describes two scenes: Jael's assassination of Sisera and the latter's mother waiting anxiously for the return of her son. Then it concludes with an acclamation of Yahweh's victory, which is

shared by those who love God. Here is the poem in its entirety
(Judg. 5)[7]:

> In Israel the warriors let their hair loose,
> in Israel they presented voluntary offering for the
>   war.
> Blessed be Yahweh!

> Listen, O kings; pay attention, O´princes,
> To Yahweh will I sing.
> To Yahweh, the God of Israel, will I offer praise.

> When you went forth from Seir, O Yahweh,
> when you came from the camp of Edom,
> the earth trembled,
> the heavens reeled and the clouds poured down rain.
> The mountains rocked before Yahweh,
> before Yahweh—the God of Israel.

> In the days of Shamgar the son of Anath,
> in the days of Yael, caravans ceased
> and travelers wandered through the byways.
> There were no leaders in Israel
> until I, Deborah, awoke and arose as a mother of
>   Israel.

> They went after new gods,
> and war was upon them.
> There was hardly a shield or a spear
> for forty thousand men in Israel!

> My heart is with the leaders of Israel
> among the people who came willingly.
> Blessed be Yahweh!

> Those who go riding on white asses,
> those who walk by the way, meditate!
> Hear the voice of those who divide the plunder
> near the watering place:

they sing the favors God has done to Israel
when the people of Yahweh march down to the gates.

Wake up, Deborah, wake up!
Wake up, wake up and begin to sing.
Arise, Barak!
And bring your songs, son of Ahinoam.

Let the survivors of the people rule over their oppres-
        sors!
May Yahweh be with me, stronger than the valiant!
Your roots, O Ephraim, are in Amalek;
your brother Benjamin is behind you among your
        army.
From Machir the commanders marched down;
from Zebulun the leaders bearing the brass staff.

The leaders of Issachar are with Deborah.
Issachar is with Barak;
the people rushed forth following
their footsteps into the plain.

There were long talks among the clans of Reuben.
Why did you choose to remain in your folds
listening to the flute among the flock?
The clans of Reuben could not decide.

Galaad remained on the other side of the Jordan,
and Dan, why did you remain in your ships?
Asher has remained on the sea coasts;
he is quiet in his ports.

Zabulun, in turn, has scorned death;
Napthtali went up to the battlefield, too.
The kings came to fight; the kings of Canaan fought
        at Taanach,
near the waters of Megiddo,
but they got no silver.

From the heavens the stars fought, from their orbits
they found against Sisera.
The torrent Kishon dragged them away, the cold tor-
    rent,
the torrent Kishon.
March on, without fear, my soul!

Hoofs of horses shake the ground:
the galloping, galloping of his horses.
Cursed be Meroz, said the angel of Yahweh,
cursed be it,
cursed be its inhabitants,
for it came not to the aid of Yahweh, not like the
    heroes.

Blessed among women be Yael, wife of Heber the
    Kenite,
among the women who dwell in tents,
blessed may you be!
He asked for water, she gave him milk;
in the cup of honor she served him cream.

She put her hand to the peg and with her right hand
took the hammer of a workman.
She struck Sisera, crushed his head,
pierced and shattered his temple.
He collapsed at her feet
and there he fell, and lay still.

Sisera's mother looks out of the window,
and she cries out behind the lattice:
Why is his chariot late in coming?
Why is his chariot delayed?
The wisest of her women answers and says:
Surely they are dividing the plunder —
one captive, two captives for each warrior;
colored cloths for Sisera as booty,
colored cloths twice adorned with raised embroidery
    for a scarf.

So may all your enemies perish, O Yahweh,
but may your friends be like the brilliant sun!
And there was peace in the land for forty years.

PRAYING WITH DEBORAH

Prayer Experience

• To let the prayer experience flow more smoothly, read the instructions ahead of time until you become more familiar with the process. Then proceed at your own pace and make your own adaptation if you wish.

• Or record the instructions on a cassette recorder, pausing whenever the three dotted marks (. . .) appear. This way you can follow your own pace during the prayer process.

• If you plan to use this with a group, have someone lead the prayer process.

1. Breath-Prayer. Be still and become aware of your own breathing . . . Close your eyes so that you can focus your attention inwardly . . . Allow the rhythm of your own breathing to quiet your whole body and inner being . . . Let your breathing sweep your mind and clear it of thoughts and distractions . . . While breathing in, lift up your heart to God while saying the following phrase, "Blessed be Yahweh" . . . While doing so, become aware of God's presence entering your body and whole being as you breathe in . . . and while breathing out, repeat to yourself the words "My God, I praise you." (You may choose your own mantra or phrase if you wish.) . . . As you breathe out, repeating the second part of the mantra to yourself, allow all your tensions, anxieties, and negative feelings to leave your body until slowly you feel a sense of deep relaxation. Do this for a few moments, allowing your rhythmic breathing to relax your body and to take you deeper and deeper into the center of your inner self . . . the place where you shall experience deep silence and oneness with God and yourself . . .

2. Reflective Reading. In silence, read over Deborah's prayer until you get a mental picture of what it describes.

3. Guided Imagery: Become quiet and take a few deep, slow breaths . . . Imagine yourself with Deborah and Barak after they triumphed over Sisera. Filled with thanksgiving for God's deliverance, you recall the people God sent you to help you overcome certain struggles, crises, or difficulties in your life as a leader of a community or as a parent who had to exercise certain authority and leadership the family . . . Recall the people, who like Barak and the tribes of Israel, have gone out of their way to assist you. (Try to picture these people in your mind and what they have done to assist you.) . . . What was your experience like having to make difficult decisions for the sake of the common good? What are your feelings as you recall your experiences? What images come to you? . . . Stay with these images for as long as you wish . . . Allow the Spirit to take you and lead you to wherever God wishes you to go in your guided meditation . . . Then imagine yourself leading the song of praise and thanksgiving with all the people who have helped you by your side . . . Stay with your feelings for a while . . . Then read again Deborah's Song slowly and prayerfully, adding your own words and phrases to fit your experience, or compose your own prayer of praise and thanksgiving.

4. Prayer in Action. Here are some suggestions that will help you concretize your own prayer:
- —Reflect on your own leadership qualities or potentials. Develop and use them in building up the community or family unity.
- —Cooperate with your own community or family.
- —Celebrate life by affirming yourself and others.

9

HANNAH

1 Samuel 1:1–2:10

Hannah, the Prayerful Mother

In a culture where childlessness was considered a curse and a source of shame, motherhood was the goal and fulfillment of every woman. But to the childless woman who kept her faith, God's mercy would be shown through the reversal of her barren condition. This was precisely the experience of Hannah, one of the wives of Elkanah of Ephraim and the mother of the prophet Samuel. Although she was Elkanah's preferred wife, she was childless. Even though she was taunted endlessly by Elkanah's other wife for her barren condition, she remained faithful to God in her suffering. On an annual pilgrimage to Yahweh's shrine at Shiloh, Hannah fervently prayed to God for an end to her suffering. She vowed that if she bore a son, she would dedicate him to God.

O Yahweh of hosts, if only you will have compassion on your maidservant and give me a son, I will put him in your service for as long as he lives and no razor shall touch his head (1 Sam. 1:11).

So intense was her prayer that Eli, the priest, thought she was in a drunken stupor. But she readily explained to him why and for what she was praying. Eli then blessed her for her faith. Because she believed, God answered her prayer and, when she bore a son, she named him Samuel. After weaning him, she fulfilled her vow and offered the boy Samuel in God's service at the shrine in Shiloh in the presence of Eli. Samuel would later become Israel's prophet and leader. Because Hannah generously offered God her blessing, God later gave her three sons and two daughters (1 Sam. 2:21).

Hannah's Prayer

Besides the short prayer she pronounced begging God to grant her a son, Hannah is more famous for her song of praise to God. In it she expresses how God metes out justice to all the world in accordance with divine wisdom. Such wisdom is shown in the abasement of the powerful and the exaltation of the lowly as well as in the routing of the enemies and the protection of the faithful. The prayer likewise affirms God's unique power over life and death. The themes of reversal of human fortunes and the defeat of one's enemies also appear in other psalms and in Wisdom literature.[1] Like most psalms, this prayer contains no evidence of a date of composition, although scholars contend that the allusion to the anointed king in 2:10 suggests that it was composed during the period of Israel's monarchy. Hannah's prayer is a source and prototype of Mary's Magnificat in Luke's Gospel.[2]

Here is her prayer.[3]

> My heart exults in you, Yahweh,
> I feel strong in you, my God.
> I rejoice and laugh at my enemies
> for you came with power to save me.
>
> Yahweh, you alone are holy, no one is like you;
> there is no Rock like our God.

Speak proudly no more;
no more arrogance on your lips,
for Yahweh is an all-knowing God,
who weighs the deeds of all.

The bow of the mighty is broken
but the weak are girded with strength.
The well-fed must labor for bread
but the hungry need work no more.
The childless wife has borne seven children,
but the proud mother is left alone.
Yahweh is Lord of life and death;
Yahweh brings down to the grave and raises up.

Yahweh makes poor and makes rich,
the Holy One brings low and exalts.
Yahweh lifts up the lowly from the dust,
and raises the poor from the ash heap;
they will be called to the company of princes,
and inherit a seat of honor.

The earth to its pillars belongs to Yahweh
and on them God has set the world.
Yahweh guards the steps of the faithful ones,
but the wicked perish in darkness,
for no one succeeds by one's own strength.

The enemies of Yahweh are shattered,
against them God thunders in heaven.
Yahweh rules over the whole world,
a king God will raise.
God's anointed feels strong in the Holy One.

PRAYING WITH HANNAH

Prayer Experience

• To let the prayer experience flow more smoothly, read the
instructions ahead of time until you become more familiar with

the process. Then proceed at your own pace and make your own adaptation if you wish.

• Or record the instructions on a cassette recorder, pausing whenever the three dotted marks (. . .) appear. This way you can follow your own pace during the prayer process.

• If you plan to use this with a group, have someone lead the prayer process.

1. Breath-Prayer. Be still and become aware of your own breathing . . . Close your eyes so that you can focus your attention inwardly . . . Allow the rhythm of your own breathing to quiet your whole body and inner being . . . Let your breathing sweep your mind and clear it of thoughts and distractions . . . While breathing in, lift up your heart to God and pronounce the divine name, "Yahweh, my God." . . . While doing so, become aware of God's presence entering your body and whole being as you breathe in . . . and while breathing out, repeat to yourself the words "My heart exults in you." (You may choose your own mantra or phrase if you wish.) . . . And as you breathe out, repeating the second part of the mantra to yourself, allow all your tensions, anxieties, and negative feelings to leave your body until slowly you feel a sense of deep relaxation. Do this for a few moments, allowing your rhythmic breathing to relax your body and to take you deeper and deeper into the center of your inner self . . . the place where you shall experience deep silence and oneness with God and yourself . . .

2. Memory. Recall an experience of extreme need. What was your prayer like? How did God answer your fervent prayer? Then read slowly and meditatively Hannah's prayer of praise and thanksgiving (1 Sam. 2:1–10).

3. Guided Imagery. Become quiet and take a few deep, slow breaths . . . Imagine yourself in Hannah's place. You are being taunted for your barren condition, people are laughing and scorning you. There are also those who are feeling sorry for you. Yet there are a few people who continue to love you in spite of your unfortunate situation. You are tempted to despair in your predicament. But something in you is preventing you from losing your faith and hope in God. At God's shrine, you pray fervently, pouring out your heart to Yahweh in your need and suffering. You feel light within you after having poured out the burden of your spirit. Something within tells you that God will answer your prayer . . . But you have to wait for God's time. Then the great moment of truth comes—you find out you are with child . . . You feel a new life pulsating within you, stirring in your womb . . . Filled with joy and thanksgiving, you feel like singing . . . You can't contain your own joy, you want others to share in your blessing. You recall your vow to the Lord and want to make good your promise. What greater joy will you have than to share your blessing with God? . . . What images come to you? . . . Stay with these feelings and images for as long as you wish . . . Allow the Spirit to take you and lead you to wherever God wishes you to go in your guided meditation . . . Then imagine a similar situation when God answered your fervent prayer and came to your assistance. What were your feelings? . . . Stay with your feelings for a while . . . then read again Hannah's prayer slowly and prayerfully, adding your own words and phrases to fit your experience. (As an alternative, you may use Mary's Magnificat in Luke 1:46–55 or compose your own magnificat.)

4. Prayer in Action. Here are some suggestions that will help you concretize your own prayer:

- Listen to someone who is suffering from oppression of any kind.
- Extend your help to poor mothers who are unable to feed their own children.
- Be fertile and creative emotionally and spiritually by using the gifts God has given you.

10

JUDITH

Judith, the Beautiful Widow and Heroine

Judith, the beautiful widow of Manasseh of Bethulia and the heroine of the book named after her, used her beauty to conquer fear at the time of Assyria's invasion of the countries of western Asia. The Israelites, who had initially refused to surrender to Holofernes, the Assyrian army leader, grew fearful when the latter besieged their city and cut off their water supply. They gave God a time limit in which to send rain; otherwise they planned to surrender. Judith argued against surrendering, scolding her own people for their faintheartedness, and urged them to trust in Yahweh. Then she revealed her plan to deliver the city.

After entrusting herself to God in prayer, she entered the enemy camp. Using her beauty and her intelligence as her weapons, she flattered Holofernes by promising him victory. Alone with him in a private banquet in his own tent, she seized the opportunity of the moment when Holofernes was in a drunken stupor. After praying, she took his sword, prayed a second time (13:7), then cut off his head. Placing his head in a food bag, she returned to Bethulia together with her maid. Her townspeople praised her great deed and courage (13:17–20).

The next day the Israelites defeated the leaderless Assyrians following Judith's plan of attack. Triumphant, they celebrated for three months. Judith's fame spread all throughout the land. Many men desired to marry her, but she chose to live alone for the rest of her long life. Before her death, she freed her maid and distributed her property.[1] Judith was buried beside Manasseh and mourned for seven days.

Judith's image is a "composite of all the women who have saved Israel in the past by their piety, wisdom, and action."[2] Her story is a real tribute to all the women whose memory ancient Israel revered for their courage in saving Israel at a time when the leaders were unable to meet the challenges of their faith.[3]

Judith's Prayers: A Profession of Faith

Although Judith's deed—assassination and achieving her end by implicit seduction—has often been judged harshly, her critics fail to grasp the lesson conveyed by the writer: that the Israelites should trust in God to protect them.[4] Following the Deuteronomic historical tradition, the character of the heroes or their methods of war were not the object of a strict moral evaluation.[5] God saves through the deeds of humans who act as humans. The theology conveyed by the book and synthesized in Judith's prayer is this: Yahweh is "the God of the depressed, the helper of the lowly, the avenger of the helpless, the protector of the contemptible, the savior of the desperate" (9:11). Though the book is undated, the theological content, which emphasizes the hope of deliverance from foreign invaders and obedience to the law, suggests that it belongs to the Maccabean period.[6]

Here are the two prayers attributed to Judith. The first, which appears in 9:2–14, was her prayer before she entered enemy camp, while the second prayer, which appears in 16:1–17, was the hymn of thanksgiving she intoned after God delivered her and her people from their enemy.

1. Prayer Invoking God's Help (9:2–14). In this prayer which begins by recalling the violence, indignity, and defilement that her people, especially the women, have suffered in the past at the hands of their enemies, Judith asks three things of Yahweh. First, that God may hear her widow's prayer (9:4); second, that God may break the Assyrians' military might (9:8); and the final request, that God may give her strength and courage to defeat the Assyrians by the "deceit of her lips" (9:10).

Pulling on ashes and sackcloth, Judith invoked aloud the following prayer at the same moment when incense was being offered in God's temple at Jerusalem:

> Lord, God of my father Simeon,
> you placed a sword in his hand to punish the foreigners who did violence to a young girl.
> For they had abused her,
> uncovering her body to shame her and violating her womb to dishonor her.
> They did this though you said:
> This shall not be done.
> Because of this you handed over their leaders to be slain and their bed, reddened because of their deceit,
> was left red with their blood.
> You struck down the slaves with their leaders and the leaders themselves with their servants.
> You handed over their women to rape,
> their daughters to slavery and all their possessions to be shared among your favored sons who were filled with horror at this defilement of their blood and invoked your help.
>
> O God, my God, listen to me, a widow!
> It is you who made all things past,
> what is present and what is yet to come.
> It is you who consider things present and to come.
> Those things which you decided have been realized.
> The things you have planned have presented themselves saying:

Here we are.
In truth, all your ways are prepared and your decision
     is known from the beginning of time.

Therefore see what a great multitude these Assyrians
     make with their army,
how they pride themselves on their horses and their
     cavalrymen.
They have placed great pride in the strength of their
     foot soldiers
and their trust in their shields, javelins, bows and
     arrows.
But they do not recognize that you, Lord,
decide the outcome of wars.
Lord is your name;
wipe out their force with your power,
and in your anger overthrow their superiority;
for they intend to profane your Sanctuary,
to defile your Tabernacle where your glorious Name
     resides,
to overturn by force the horn of your altar.

Consider their pride,
let your anger fall on their heads
and give to my hands, the hands of a widow,
the strength necessary for what I have decided.
By my lying lips punish the slave with his master and
     the master with his servant;
put an end to their arrogance by the hand of a
     woman.

Truly your strength is not in number
nor your power in strong men
for you are a God of the humble,
the defender of the little ones,
the support of the weak,
the protector of the abandoned,
the savior of those in despair.

Yes, God of my ancestors and God of the heritage
    of Israel,
Ruler of the heavens and the earth,
Creator of the waters,
King of all creation,
listen to my prayer.

Give me tempting words to wound and kill those who
    have conceived cruel designs against your Cov-
    enant,
your consecrated House,
Mount Sion and the House which belongs to your
    children.

Make the nation and all the tribes know that you are
    God,
all-powerful and strong,
and that, apart from you,
there is no other protector for the people of Israel.

2. The Song of Judith (16:1–17). As a liturgical poem, it opens
with a hymnic introduction (1–2) in which Judith calls the people to worship and proclaims God as the real victor and deliverer.[7] The main portion of the poem is a descriptive narrative
of the events that happened. Judith speaks of the Assyrian
threat while another voice narrates Judith's triumph (3–12). The
favors Judith asked God for in her first prayer have been granted
as recounted in this poem. The last four verses are a hymnic
conclusion in which Judith sings praises to God (v. 13) and calls
all creation to join her in her song. Here is the entire hymn:[8]

Sing a song to my God with tambourines,
sing in honor of God with cymbals.
Compose for God a psalm of praise.
Exalt and bless God's Name!
The Lord is truly a God who crushes war,
who encamps in the midst of the people
for the Holy One has snatched me from the hand of
    those who pursued me.

The Assyrian came from the mountains of the north.
He came with the myriads of his army,
his soldiers have filled the torrents
and his cavalry covered the hills.
He wanted to burn my land,
to kill the young men by the sword,
to destroy my children at the breast,
to hand over my little ones to slaughter
and to rape my young maidens.

The Lord Almighty has driven them back by the hand
        of a woman.
Their hero has not been overcome by young warriors;
he was not struck down by the sons of the Titans,
or laid low by any great giants.
But it is Judith, the daughter of Merari
who by the beauty of her face has defeated him.
For the relief of the oppressed in Israel
she took off her widow's robes,
anointed her face with perfume,
put a jewelled band around her hair,
and put on a linen dress in order to seduce him.
Her sandals delighted his eyes,
her beauty captivated his soul,
and the scimitar cut through his neck.

The Persians trembled with fear at her boldness,
and the Medes were upset by her daring.
Then my oppressed people shouted for joy;
my weak ones cried out,
the enemy was terrified;
they raised their voices; the enemy took to flight.
The children of young women pierced them through
        and struck them down like fugitives,
and so the enemy perished in a battle arranged by
        God.

I will sing to my God a new song;
Lord, you are great and glorious,

wonderfully strong, invincible!
May the whole of your creation serve you,
for you spoke and all things were,
you sent forth your spirit and all things came into
      being;
No one can resist your voice.
For the mountains with the waters will be shaken to
      their foundations,
the rocks will melt like wax before you,
but to those who fear you
you will always show mercy.

The fragrance of any sacrifice is little to please you
and the holocausts of fatted animals
are as nothing before you,
but the one who fears the Lord is forever great,
Woe to the nations which rise up against my people;
The Lord Almighty will punish them in the day of
      judgment,
with fire and worms under their skin,
and they will keep on weeping,
suffering forever.

PRAYING WITH JUDITH

Prayer Experience

• To let the prayer experience flow more smoothly, read the instructions ahead of time until you become more familiar with the process. Then proceed at your own pace and make your own adaptation if you wish.

• Or record the instructions on a cassette recorder, pausing whenever the three dotted marks (...) appear. This way you can follow your own pace during the prayer process.

• If you plan to use this with a group, have someone lead the prayer process.

1. Breath-Prayer. Be still and become aware of your own breathing ... Close your eyes so that you can focus your attention inwardly . . . Allow the rhythm of your own breathing to quiet your whole body and inner being . . . Let your breathing sweep your mind and clear it of thoughts and distractions . . . While breathing in, lift up your heart to God and pronounce the divine name, "O God, my God" (or "Yahweh, my God") . . . While doing so, become aware of God's presence entering your body and whole being as you breathe in . . . and while breathing out, repeat to yourself the words "Listen to my prayer" (or "My heart exults in you"). (You may choose your own mantra or phrase if you wish.) . . . As you breathe out, repeating the second part of the mantra to yourself, allow all your tensions, anxieties, and negative feelings to leave your body until slowly you feel a sense of deep relaxation. Do this for a few moments, allowing your rhythmic breathing to relax your body and to take you deeper and deeper into the center of your inner self . . . the place where you shall experience deep silence and oneness with God and yourself . . .

2. Prayer Using One's Memory or Imagination. Do either of the following prayer suggestions:

• *Memory.* Recall an experience of great difficulty or danger in your life or in your loved one's life (such as serious illness, loss of job resulting in great financial difficulty, etc.) . . . Where was God in your life? . . . What was your prayer like (if you prayed at all?) How did God answer your fervent prayer? . . . Then read slowly and meditatively Judith's first prayer (9:2–14). (Like the other prayers of lament in the Psalms and in Wisdom literature, this prayer is suited for times of doubt, difficulty, crisis, etc.)

Recall the time after you overcame the above experience . . . What were your feelings? . . . What was your prayer like? . . . What was your image of God? . . . Try to enter into your feelings about life and about God, then read prayerfully Judith's second prayer (16:1–17).

• *Guided Imagery.* Become quiet and take a few deep, slow breaths . . . Imagine yourself in Judith's place . . . The people around you have given up hope, but with your words you help them to recover hope and faith in God as savior . . . Mustering all the courage from your soul and relying only on God, you try to enter enemy camp, bluffing your way through by using your charm and intelligence. ... Though fearful, you know God is with you. ... The next thing you realize is that you're returning to Bethulia from the enemy camp. ... Everything happened in a flash. ... You still can't believe you were successful in your mission. ... You try to recall what happened. ... You saw yourself in Holofernes' tent pretending to have a good time with him. ... He was getting drunker by the minute. ... Then you saw the golden opportunity you had been waiting for. ... The enemy was lying in his tent in a drunken stupor, unsuspecting of your motives and vulnerable in your hands. ... You were affirming yourself that you could overcome him. ... Your heart was racing within you and you could hear its every beat. ... You looked around and saw the enemy's sword in its sheath. ... Without thinking for a moment, you grabbed it and in two strong strokes you severed the enemy's head with the force coming from your righteous anger. ... Then you swiftly put the enemy's head in your food bag and left the tent with your maid in the darkness of the night.

Now you're on your way back to your own town, still dazed at how you have achieved your mission in a flash, yet it seemed like the night was endless as you waited for the opportunity to catch the enemy at his weakest position. ... As you reach your town, you see the people gathered. ... keeping vigil and waiting for your arrival. ... expressions of relief and anxious anticipation painted all over their faces. ... Then you hold the bloody bag up for everyone to see. ... The men come forward to remove the enemy's head from the bag to see for themselves that the enemy has truly been conquered. ... Some are looking away, content to know that you are back safely, while others are crying for joy and thanksgiving. ... The people's faith has been restored.

You decide to leave the crowd to be alone ... to sort out your feelings and most of all to thank God for using you as an instrument to save others. ... What images come to you now? ... What feelings are surfacing from within you? ... Stay with these feelings and images for as long as you wish. ... Allow the Spirit to take you and lead you to wherever God wishes you to go in your guided meditation. ... Then imagine a similar situation when you were asked to do a difficult yet important mission — a situation when God used you as an instrument to help others. . . . What were your feelings then? What are your feelings now? . . . Stay with your feelings for a while . . . then read again Judith's first prayer silently to yourself, allowing the words to penetrate your being . . . Then recall the time when you experienced success in your difficult mission. . . . What were your feelings then? . . . What are your feelings and realizations now? . . . What images come to you now? Stay with the images and feelings for a while, then slowly and prayerfully read Judith's second prayer, adding your own words and phrases to fit your experience.

3. Prayer in Action. Here are some suggestions that will help you concretize your own prayer:

— Become aware of the oppressive structures that exist in your own home, community, society, and world.
— Be involved in programs that raise the consciousness of others regarding the plight of the oppressed and the marginalized.
— Practice making everyday decisions with self-confidence and trust in God.

Further Recommendations. Read the Book of Judith.

11

ESTHER

Esther the Queen

Esther, whose Jewish name was Hadassah,[1] is the central figure and heroine of the book bearing her name.[2] The setting of her fictional story is the diaspora (the Jewish settlements outside of Israel).[3] From among throngs of lovely maidens, Hadassah was chosen by Ahasuerus, king of Persia, to replace the deposed queen Vashti, who had refused to submit herself to the indignity of displaying her beauty before the royal courtiers[4] (1:11). In choosing Esther, the king had no idea that she was a Jewess.[5] When she became queen, she was given the Persian name Esther.

Esther's cousin Mordecai, who had reared her and was somehow responsible for her present position, had earlier discovered a plot against the king's life by two palace eunuchs, but he had never been rewarded for the deed. Furthermore, he had also earned the wrath of Haman, a palace insider, for his refusal to bow to him out of religious scruples. In fact, Haman hated not only Mordecai but the Jewish people as well because of their religious practices. Haman used his position to successfully request the king to issue a decree that all Jews in the kingdom be slain. He also planned to have Mordecai hanged.

Aware of Haman's murderous plot against the Jews, Mordecai requested Esther to appeal to the king on behalf of her people. Quietly she first asked her people to join her in prayer and fasting that the planned pogrom (officially organized massacre) may not succeed. Then she took the risk of approaching the king even without being summoned. Although her heart was filled with fear, she looked radiant and her face depicted love and joy. The king's initial reaction to her appearance before him was anger, but her beauty and charm helped her win his confidence and affection. His anger was changed to gentleness (15:8). Delighted with her beauty, the king asked her what she wished to have from his kingdom. Her only response was to have him and Haman as her guests at a banquet she herself would prepare, and there she would reveal her answer to his question. At the banquet, when she was asked again by the king what she wanted, she gave the same response: to have him and Haman as guests at another banquet she would prepare. It was at this second banquet that she finally revealed to the king an enemy plot against her and her people, and Haman's role in it.

The same dread that Haman had so lightly cast upon the Jews was now falling upon himself. However, since the king could not revoke a decree he himself had signed and marked with his royal seal, he gave Esther and Mordecai authority to write a letter to the entire kingdom in his name, giving the Jews in each city the right to assemble and avenge themselves against their enemies. At every place where the edict was read, there was rejoicing and festivity. Many people of other nationalities were seized with fear of the Jews and embraced Judaism (8:11). Now the tables were turned. Esther was successful in delivering her people from an officially sanctioned genocide, giving the Jews in the entire kingdom reason to thank and praise God for their deliverance. To commemorate the event, the Feast of Purim has become a traditional celebration in Israel.[6]

Esther's Prayer

To provide religious motifs to the book, the Greek author of the Book of Esther inserts two prayers: one attributed to Mordecai, the other to Esther. In this chapter we shall focus only on Esther's prayer, which highlights first of all her own desperate situation and her plea that God may answer her cry for help. The prayer belongs to the genre of lament and combines elements of individual and national lament—she is "alone"; the nation has "sinned" (14:17) and God's fidelity to the promises is at stake (14:20).[7] If Yahweh fails to intervene, idolatry will only flourish. In the prayer Esther makes a profession of faith that truly reflects Israel's conviction of God's goodness.

Burdened with great responsibility to save her own people and wearing garments of distress and mourning at the prospect of her own death and that of her people, Esther prayed to the God of Israel in these words (14:4-19):[8]

> My Lord, our King, the only God,
> come to my rescue,
> I am alone and have no help but you.
>
> Through my own choice I am endangering my life.
> As a child I was wont to hear from the people of the
>   land of my forebears
> that you, O Lord, chose Israel from among all peo-
>   ples,
> and our ancestors from among their ancestors
> to be your lasting heritage;
> that you did for them all that you have promised.
>
> But we have sinned,
> and for this you have handed us over to our enemies;
> we have worshiped their gods,
> but you, O Lord, are just.
> Dissatisfied with our bitter servitude,
> they made a pact with their idols
> to abolish what you have decreed,
> to blot out your heritage,

to shut the mouths that give you praise,
to quench the glory of your house and your altar
and instead to let the pagans sing the praise of worth-
    less idols,
and idolize forever a king of flesh.

Do not give up your scepter, O Lord,
to nonexistent beings.
Never let them gloat over our ruin,
but turn their designs against themselves
and make an example of your chief enemy.

Remember us, Lord;
reveal yourself in the time of our calamity.
Give me courage, King of gods and master of all
    power.
Make my words persuasive when I face the lion;
turn his heart against our enemy,
that the latter and his like may be brought to their
    end.

Save us by your hand;
help me who am alone and have none but you, O
    Lord.

You know everything;
you know how I hate honor from the goddess,
how I loathe the bed of the uncircumcised and of any
    foreigner.

You know I am here under constraint,
that I loathe the diadem about my brow
when I appear in public;
as a filthy rag I loathe it
and do not wear it in private.

Your handmaid has never eaten at Haman's table,
nor taken pleasure in royal banquets,
nor drunk the wine offered to their gods.

Neither has your handmaid found pleasure
from the day of her promotion till now except in you,
Lord God of Abraham.

O God, more powerful than all,
hear the voice of those in despair;
save us from the evil one's power,
and deliver me from my fear.

PRAYING WITH ESTHER

Prayer Experience

• To let the prayer experience flow more smoothly, read the instructions ahead of time until you become more familiar with the process. Then proceed at your own pace and make your own adaptation if you wish.

• Or record the instructions on a cassette recorder, pausing whenever the three dotted marks (...) appear. This way you can follow your own pace during the prayer process.

• If you plan to use this with a group, have someone lead the prayer process.

1. Breath-Prayer. Be still and become aware of your own breathing ... Close your eyes so that you can focus your attention inwardly ... Allow the rhythm of your own breathing to quiet your whole body and inner being ... Let your breathing sweep your mind and clear it of thoughts and distractions ... While breathing in, lift up your heart to God and pronounce the divine name, "Yahweh, my God". . . While doing so, become aware of God's presence entering your body and whole being as you breathe in ... and while breathing out, repeat to yourself the words "Give me courage." (You may choose your own mantra or phrase if you wish.) ... As you breathe out, repeating the second part of the mantra to yourself, allow all your tensions, anxieties, and negative feelings to leave your body until slowly you feel a sense of deep relaxation. Do this for a few moments, allowing your rhythmic breathing to relax your body and to take you deeper and deeper into the center of your inner self . . . the place where you shall experience deep silence and oneness with God and yourself . . .

2. Prayer Using One's Memory or Imagination. Do either of the following prayer suggestions:

• *Memory.* Recall an experience of great difficulty and need or an experience of betrayal. . . . Where was God in your life? . . . What was your prayer like? . . . Try to enter into your feelings of distress and weakness as you called upon God for help. . . . Then read slowly and meditatively Esther's prayer of lament (14:4-19). How did you feel after you had poured your heart out to God? . . . Remain in silence for a while. . . . Then in your own words express to God your own sentiments.

• *Guided Imagery.* Become quiet and take a few deep, slow breaths . . . Imagine yourself in Esther's place. You are aware of someone plotting against you to destroy you and your people. . . . You alone are in a position to do something against this evil plot. . . . You dread having to risk your life and reputation to do what is necessary—to reveal the painful truth. . . . What feelings are surfacing from within you? . . . Stay with these feelings and images for as long as you wish . . . Allow the Spirit to take you and lead you to wherever God wishes you to go in your guided meditation. . . . Then imagine a similar situation you have experienced in the past . . . You were aware of evil disguising itself as good but people were not seeing what you saw. . . . You had to convince them to see the truth of the situation or the structures of oppression and injustice present in the situation. . . . What were your feelings about your responsibility? . . . What action did you take? . . . What was the result of your action? . . . While recalling the personal experience, read prayerfully Esther's prayer of lament (14:4-19), adding your own words and phrases to fit your experience as you please.

3. Prayer in Action. Here are some suggestions that will help you concretize your own prayer:

—Become aware of structures of oppression and injustice that exist in your own community and society and in the

relationships between first- and third-world countries.
— Always seek the truth even if the process is painful.

Further Recommendation. Read the Book of Esther.

12

SUSANNA
Daniel 13

Susanna the Accused

Susanna is the heroine of the story in the thirteenth chapter of the Book of Daniel.[1] The setting of her story is Babylon. Trained by her pious parents in the law of Moses, this young, refined, and beautiful daughter of Hilkiah became the wife of Joakim, a rich and influential person in whose house the local court sat (13:1-6). Because of her beauty, she became the object of the lustful desire of two elders or magistrates of the court. At the first opportunity that they found her alone, they trapped her in the garden of her home while she was bathing and threatened to accuse her of adultery unless she submitted herself to them (13:15-21). Susanna refused their demands (13:22-23) and was falsely accused, hastily tried, and unjustly condemned to death (13:24-41). Even her family and friends who believed in her innocence were powerless against the wicked elders. Completely trusting in God, she raised her tearful eyes to heaven and prayed to God for assistance.

197

In response to her prayer, God sent the young Daniel to help her (13:42-46) by inspiring him to question the judgment of the court. He refused to accept the verdict and proclaimed that he would not have any part in the death of the accused. He reminded the court that they could not condemn anyone without due process and in the absence of clear evidence against the accused (13:48-49). He demanded that the case be reopened and a proper investigation and trial be conducted.

Detecting their falsehood, Daniel interrogated the two elders separately and proved their guilt and evil intentions. Susanna was vindicated and her two detractors were executed in her place. The story ends with Susanna's parents and husband praising God and with Daniel's reputation as a wise and discerning judge spreading among the Jewish people.

Susanna's Prayer: The Plea of an Innocent Victim

The inseparable connection of confidence and humility is expressed in the prayer of poor and powerless people like Susanna.[2] Completely trusting in the Lord, she raised her tearful eyes to heaven in silence and sorrow (13:35). At first no words came from her lips. Defenseless, in mortal danger and completely deprived of a right to due process, she had only her faith and hope in God—a God she believed always listened to the cries of the poor. As she was being led to her death, all she could utter was a short and simple prayer—a prayer that pierced the heavens and evoked an immediate response from God. She cried out to God in these words (13:42-43):

> Eternal God,
> nothing is hidden from you;
> you know all things before they came to be.
> You know that these men have testified falsely
>   against me.
> Would you let me die,
> though I am not guilty
> of all their malicious charges?

PRAYING WITH SUSANNA

Prayer Experience

• To let the prayer experience flow more smoothly, read the instructions ahead of time until you become more familiar with the process. Then proceed at your own pace and make your own adaptation if you wish.

• Or record the instructions on a cassette recorder, pausing whenever the three dotted marks (. . .) appear. This way you can follow your own pace during the prayer process.

• If you plan to use this with a group, have someone lead the prayer process.

1. Breath-Prayer. Be still and become aware of your own breathing . . . Close your eyes so that you can focus your attention inwardly . . . Allow the rhythm of your own breathing to quiet your whole body and inner being . . . Let your breathing sweep your mind and clear it of thoughts and distractions . . . While breathing in, lift up your heart to God and pronounce the divine name, "My God, my God" (or "Eternal God") . . . While doing so, become aware of God's presence entering your body and whole being as you breathe in . . . and while breathing out, repeat to yourself the words "Do not abandon me" (or "Nothing is hidden from you"). (You may choose your own mantra or phrase if you wish.) . . . As you breathe out, repeating the second part of the mantra to yourself, allow all your tensions, anxieties, and negative feelings to leave your body until slowly you feel a sense of deep relaxation. Do this for a few moments, allowing your rhythmic breathing to relax your body and to take you deeper and deeper into the center of your inner self . . . the place where you shall experience deep silence and oneness with God and self . . .

2. Prayer Using One's Memory or Imagination. Do either of the following prayer suggestions:

• *Memory.* Recall an experience when you were accused falsely of wrongdoing or when false information was spread about you, affecting your career or relationships. . . . What were your feelings then? . . . What are your feelings now? . . . Where was God in your life? . . . What was your prayer like? . . . Feel your feelings again. . . . Then let Susanna's prayer be your own (14:4-19), adding your own words and phrases according to the Spirit's inspiration in you.

   • *Imagination.* Become quiet and take a few deep, slow breaths . . . Imagine yourself in Susanna's place facing trial before the elders. . . . Your family and friends are there with you, weeping and helpless as false accusations are flung against you by the two elders. . . . You remain speechless and in distress. . . . You are not even given the opportunity to be heard. . . . Because of their reputable position in the community, the people believe their every word. . . . They hastily condemn you to death. . . . Crying aloud to God, you utter the following prayer:

> "Eternal God, nothing is hidden from you; you know all things before they come to be. You know that these men have testified falsely against me. Woud you let me die, though I am not guilty of all their malicious charges?"

You begin to feel relieved when finally one person among the whole assembly, a young man whom you have not met before, stands up to defend you. As he speaks, you begin to feel a sense of hope and confidence that your situation will be changed. . . . This man is speaking with conviction and wisdom and is reminding the elders that they have desecrated the law for condemning you without due process and in the absence of clear evidence. . . . The whole assembly are ashamed of themselves and are willing to reopen the case. . . . Suddenly you realize that you're now free and the ones who falsely accused you are now being led to their own death. . . . You thank the young man who came to your rescue and pursued the truth. Your heart is filled with thanksgiving to God for answering your prayer and for not allowing you to die an unjust death. . . . Your family and friends are rejoicing with you for the triumph of truth. . . . Then imagine a similar situation you have experienced in the past. . . . People gossiping or spreading false information about you. . . . How did you deal with your painful experience? . . . What were your feelings? . . . Have you forgiven the people who have hurt you? . . . As you recall the painful experience, entrust everything to God from whom nothing is hidden and who knows all things before they come to be. . . . Put these people who have hurt you in God's hand. . . . Beg that God may give you grace to fully forgive them and that God may heal your wounded past. . . . Then pray your own words of trust and thanksgiving to God.

3. Prayer in Action. Here are some suggestions that will help you to concretize your own prayer:

—Always seek and speak the truth.
—Come to the defense of the poor and the oppressed.
—Listen to someone who has been falsely accused of wrong-doing or ostracized by others because of his or her commitment to truth.
—Visit political prisoners.

CONCLUSION

We have just reflected on the lives and spirituality of a few of the biblical women of antiquity and the challenges they continue to pose to us today through the experiences of women in the Third World and in Asia. They not only challenge us to reassess the way we understand our faith and our relationship with God; they also urge us to put our faith into action in response to the many disturbing parallels we see between their lives and experiences and those of today's women.

Out of our discussion of the spirituality of women in the Old Testament, we have seen women who were considered obscure and were negative models of spirituality (because of their shady background, race, or socio-economic class) as new paradigms of faith. They are like "hidden treasures" who are being discovered but whose luster is still covered by the darkness of ignorance and prejudice that continue to prevail in the minds and hearts of many people. Although their lives are stark reminders of the ongoing struggles of today's women, especially those from the Third World—such as the abused domestic helpers, prostituted women, and women struggling out of their poverty and ignorance—their relationship with the Divine nonetheless awakens faith and inspires courage, action, and the spirit of solidarity in us who are willing to take up their challenge more seriously.

Thus Hagar, Rahab, Jephthah's daughter, Ruth and Naomi, Abigail, and the unnamed women in the Books of Kings are no longer strangers to us but are our foresisters showing us the way along our faith journey. They show us the path to true wisdom and holiness. They challenge us to put our faith into action and to speak God's liberating word to women who are still locked up in their own dungeons of fear, prejudice, ignorance, and lack of self-worth.

In equal measure, the prayers of women in the Old Testament in the second part of this book have reminded us that biblical women were in their own way eloquent not only in word but also in deed. Their effectiveness and success as leaders did not lie in their political adroitness or influence but in their deep faith and conviction in God's mercy, guidance, and protection. Such faith was demonstrated to us by Deborah, Judith, and Esther, as each led her people at different biblical periods out of danger or possible extinction. We also saw in our reading that women like Miriam were prophets who stood between God and the people as communicators of the divine message to the people and as articulators before God of the people's joys, triumphs, sorrows, sufferings, needs, and hopes. The prayers of women like Hannah and Susanna were equally moving in their simplicity, brevity, honesty, and directness. Coming out of the depths of their need and misery, their words pierced the heavens and evoked a compassionate response from God.

These women, whether they were influential or not, named or unnamed, with or without a position in society, are speaking to us today about who we are as women of faith and where we are as persons in our modern world. Through our re-reading of Scripture, we have shed light on the situation and condition of women then and now. Yet as this book ends, we are also left with questions to ponder, some of which are disturbing or have only tentative answers. We continue to ask why there is continued subjugation of women in spite of the advancement of societies and civilizations and people's growth in consciousness. Why do women themselves discriminate against women? If feminism is seen as a justice issue, why is the church slow to promote it? We also ask what the challenges of feminist theology are in the ongoing growth of human consciousness and in faith development.

Although feminism in general, and feminist theology in North America and Europe in particular, have tried to address these questions in an attempt to represent and advance the cause of women, it cannot claim to speak for all women the world over because experiences and cultures differ despite recognized commonalities. For instance, in North America, there is now the rise of the "womanists" among African-American women and the "mujeristas" among Hispanics.[1] The stress of growth in consciousness in each ethnic group differs because of their situation and the cultural values important to them. As such, the philosophical aspects of cultural differences and their implications have to be considered. For instance, according to Dr. Carolyn Jacobs, the European-American group would stress the value of "person-to-object"; the African, African-American and Hispanic groups focus more on the "person-to-person" value; and the Native Americans, Asian Americans, and Asians would generally stress the "person-to-group" value.[2] Along these lines it could be said that for Filipina women, the accent would be more a combination of the "person-to-person" and "person-to-group" values due to the Spanish influence in the Filipino culture and the Philippines' location in Asia.

Jacobs elaborated on the philosophical aspects of cultural differences by explaining that for European Americans, the person's highest value would lie in the area of what is acquired, such as credentials, achievements, travels. Thus for them, it is important to know the person in terms of status, roles, occupation, and achievements in order to know how one might relate to the other. Because the value is "person-to-object," there is a tendency to think in a dichotomized or "either-or" way. Thus European-American women have successfully advanced their cause by getting into the academe, higher education, and theological seminaries in order that their voices may be heard. As such, they have contributed much insight to the ongoing debate and discussion regarding the place of women in church and society. They tend to be more confrontative in dealing with issues and situations than are women from other cultures.

The stress of African-American, Hispanic and Asian cultures on either "person-to-person" or "person-to-group" values makes their approach different. For the African, African-American, and Hispanic groups, the approach would take the path of relationships because the encounter with the other is given more importance. It is within the context of a "person-to-person" relationship that women's issues for these groups can be effectively advanced, not through debates or confrontations. This is because they have to deal with a lot of "machis" in their culture.

For Native Americans, Asian Americans, and Asians, the

approach would be totally different due to the cultures' stress on "person-to-group" values. Their voice tends to be more collective, and they put their highest value on the cohesiveness of the group. Because of the strong emphasis on the "familial" or "environmental" self, the individual self is lost as the group deals with coming together as one voice on one issue or as "one mind and one heart speaking with one voice."[3]

Thus, as a consequence of the differences in philosophical underpinnings, perspectives and ways of knowing and relating would also vary. For instance, the path to growth in consciousness for third-world women (either Hispanic or Asian backgrounds) can effectively be promoted through "experience-reflection-action-reflection" as a small basic community or as a "solidarity" group. Their common experience as women becomes a strong element of bonding, oneness, and support — and the impetus for a transformation in consciousness. In applying the stories of biblical women to this method, women who experience prejudice because of their gender come together to reflect on their experience and understand it against the background of the biblical women of antiquity. Their insights and reflections are further enfleshed by putting them into action. The process is enhanced by returning together as a group to reflect on their feelings and learnings after having concretized their prayer and reflection. It is important for these groups to see connections and parallels between their experiences and situation and those of the biblical women and to appropriate the stories of our biblical foresisters as their own. This can empower them and can bring them to deepening faith and awareness of their capacity to change their lot and awaken others to their dignity as human persons. This process awakens them to the basic reality that all of humanity is one and transformation can happen when there is oneness.

Although the Euro-Americans have taken a lot of initiatives in raising the consciousness of women, there may be a need to grow more in the awareness that their experience need not necessarily be taken as the standard for all women regardless of cultures. Considering that the world is becoming more multicultural, the challenge for all, especially for the Euro-American groups, is to be continually open and to listen to the voices of women from different cultures. This way each group can learn from others. Perhaps, the invitation is for them to come up with their own challenges as to how the "person-to-object" emphasis could concretely be redefined so they may be in greater solidarity and oneness with women from all cultures.

Two of the five interrelated postulates[4] in communication from an Asian perspective pick up the theme of oneness and transformation of consciousness. These postulates are applicable for all regardless of culture. One postulate says that everything is related, integrated, and united. Spirituality, for instance, emphasizes the oneness of the universe. As such, discrepancies and dichotomies do not exist because what one may think as disorder from one perspective may be order in another perspective, and whatever happens to anyone will affect somebody else because no one exists in a vacuum. There is interpenetrating unity in everything. Thus chaos, which is symbolized by a question mark, can be seen as a beautiful pattern from another perspective when a series of question marks is put together to create a paisley or "kashimiri" design. In other words, from a "microscopic" dimension there might be chaos, but from a "macroscopic" dimension, there is order and design.

The other postulate puts forth the goal of communication, which is the transformation of consciousness. From the Asian perspective, there is no such thing as "human" consciousness as such because all that exists has consciousness. Therefore, there is only one consciousness, which is evolutionary in nature and has different levels of vibration. Thus from today's perspective the consciousness of the women of antiquity about themselves as persons would certainly look "backwards," but it is the same collective consciousness that has evolved over time with our growth in knowledge and consciousness of the human person. Thus perspectives may differ according to the cultural variables of ethnicity, age, gender, socio-economic status, and education, but it is the same collective consciousness that connects all of humanity with one another from one historical age to the next. This interpenetrating unity removes dualism, dichotomies, and "either-ors," thus making our world one.

Therefore, the challenge of our biblical foresisters for third-world Asian women is to be awakened to their own situation, to begin articulating their experience, and to act to transform their situation based on their new-found consciousness and self-definition. The paradigm for the process of conversion or transformation for women, especially third-world and Asian women, is not as much a "turning around" or a "turning against" but rather an "awakening" to one's true gift of self, which is an interpenetrating unity with the whole of humanity and with the whole of creation. In this process there is no separation or "breaking away" as the "turning around" or the "turning against" paradigm implies, but there is continued relationship with all the parts of one's being, with all of history, and with all of creation.

NOTES

INTRODUCTION

1. Gabriele Dietrich, "The Origins of the Bible Revisited: Reconstructing Women's History," paper presented at a national consultation on *Towards a Theology of Humanhood: Women's Perspective—Association of Trained Women in India and Catholic Women*, Bangalore, Nov. 1984. Now in print. Used as reference in "India: A Biblical Reflection on the National Situation" in *Asian Women Doing Theology: Report from Singapore Conference* (Hong Kong: Asian Women's Resource Centre for Culture and Theology, 1989), p. 38.

2. Rosemary Radford Ruether, *Sexism and God-Talk: Towards a Feminist Theology* (London: SCM Press, 1983), p. 63.

3. Elsa Tamez, "The Woman Who Complicated the History of Salvation" in *New Eyes for Reading*, ed. John S. Pobee and Barbel von Wartenberg-Potter (Bloomington, Ind.: Meyer Stone Books, 1987), p. 5.

4. See *Asian Women Doing Theology*, p. 38.

1. HAGAR

1. Elsa Tamez, "The Woman Who Complicated the History of Salvation" in *New Eyes for Reading: Biblical and Theological Reflections by Women from the Third World*, ed. John S. Pobee and Barbel von Wartenberg-Potter (Bloomington, Ind.: Meyer Stone, 1987), p. 6.

2. *Ibid.*, p. 7.

3. *Yahwist* and *Elohist* are two of the four sources of written documents behind the present biblical text as determined by source criticism, a method of biblical research developed over the last three centuries mainly to answer the problems of repetitions and inconsistencies especially in the first five books of the Bible. The name "Yahwist" is based on the way the source referred to God's name—

Yahweh—whereas "Elohist" is so called because of its reference to God as *Elohim*. This source contained old stories and was concerned with historical traditions. See Lawrence Boadt, *Reading the Old Testament* (New York/Mahwah, N.Y.: Paulist Press, 1984), pp. 92–106.

4. Demetrius Dumm, O.S.B., *Flowers in the Desert* (New York/ Mahwah: Paulist Press, 1987), p. 18.

5. Pauline Viviano, "Genesis" in *The Collegeville Bible Commentary* (Collegeville, Minn.: The Liturgical Press, 1989), p. 56.

6. Peter Toon and Herbert Schneider, S.J., *The Compact Bible Dictionary* (Ann Arbor: Servant Books, 1987), p. 118.

7. See Tamez, p. 7.

8. See Viviano, p. 56.

9. Sharon Pace Jeansonne, *The Women of Genesis* (Minneapolis: Fortress Press, 1991), p. 44.

10. See Tamez, p. 9.

11. Phyllis Trible, *Texts of Terror. Literary-Feminist Readings of Biblical Narratives* (Philadelphia: Fortress Press, 1984), p. 12.

12. See Tamez, p. 8.

13. Based on Hammurabi Code 146, which cites the following case: "A priestess of the rank of Naditum who is free to marry, but not to have children, gives a slave to her husband to have children by. If this concubine tries to create a sense of equality between herself and the legal wife, the wife has the right to send her back to slavery, but not to sell her to others," as cited by Tamez, p. 10. Hammurabi's Law Code is the most famous and complete of ancient law codes. It consists of 282 laws inscribed on a stone pillar by the great Babylonian king in the 18th century, B.C. See Boadt, *Reading the Old Testament*, pp. 63, 186–187.

14. See Trible, p. 13.

15. Cf. Code Ham. 146 as referred to by Tamez, p. 10.

16. See Trible, p. 15. Here Trible emphasizes that the character representing the Deity acknowledges the personhood of Hagar, which Sarai and Abram have not.

17. See Jeansonne, p. 45.

18. See Trible, p. 16.

19. *Ibid.*, p. 17.

20. See Viviano, p. 56.

21. See Trible, p. 20.

22. See Viviano, p. 60.

23. See footnote 44 of Trible, p. 33.

24. See Speiser, p. 155 as noted by Tamez, p. 11. The note also says that "the Hebrew word *msajak* means 'to play,' 'to laugh'; if it is to

mean to ridicule, to mock someone, it should be preceded by a 'b,' "
cf. Skinner, *International Critical Commentary*, Genesis (London, Edin-
burgh, 1980), p. 322.

25. Based on the Hammurabi Code 170, which also states that "no
one can change that legislation, not even the mistress of the house."
See Tamez, p. 12.

26. See Emmanuelle Testa, *Genesi* (Rome: Ed. Pauline, 1972), p.
210, as noted by Tamez, p. 12.

27. This account presents us a problem of Ishmael's age if we were
to read it as a chronological continuation of the Yahwist's account.
(According to the Yahwist source, the boy must have been seventeen
years old already.) It is obvious that the Elohistic narrator makes Ishmael a little older than Isaac because Abraham, when he says good-
bye to him, places him on the back of Hagar (v. 14) and later in the
desert she lays him beneath a bush (v. 15). Cf. Tamez, p. 11.

28. See Tamez, p. 12.

29. See Jeansonne, p. 49.

30. *Ibid.* p. 50.

31. *Ibid.*

32. See Trible, p. 27.

33. See Jeansonne, p. 52.

34. See Trible, p. 28.

35. *Ibid.*

36. *Ibid.*

37. See Tamez, p. 14.

38. *Ibid.*

39. See Deut. 21:15–17.

40. See Bernardo Hurault, *CCB* commentary, p. 61.

41. See Tamez, p. 15.

42. Among the Israelites, it is only God and no one else who deigns
to name Oneself. It is through adjectives that the God of Israel was
designated in the times of the Patriarchs. See Xavier Leon-Dufour, ed.,
Dictionary of Biblical Theology, Updated Second Edition (Manila, Philippines: St. Paul Publications, 1990), pp. 377–78.

43. *Ibid.*, p. 13.

44. *Ibid.*, p. 15.

45. One recent news report estimates around 300,000 third-world
women working as housemaids in Kuwait alone. If the numbers in other
Arab countries and affluent Asian countries are to be counted, the
statistics would reach staggering proportions.

46. According to one report, such assaults and abuses on Filipino
domestic workers reached epidemic proportions in the late '80s in

Kuwait alone, which prompted the Philippine government to temporarily halt the recruitment of Filipinos for that country.

47. I read their cases in a daily column by M. Ceres P. Doyo. It was entitled "The Lornas and Lindas in the Desert." See Doyo, "Human Face" in the *Philippine Daily Inquirer*, March 13, 1992. The writer acknowledges another *Inquirer* columnist, Rina Jimenez David, as the one who first broke the story in the Philippines by quoting from a February 8, 1992, issue of *Egyptian Gazette*.

48. The verses have been freely adapted to be inclusive. Only the words in between [ ] were changed.

2. RAHAB

1. In religious harlotry, male and female prostitutes were regarded as holy persons (*qadesh, qedeshah*) and as members of a special religious caste. See John E. Steinmueller and Kathryn Sullivan, eds., *Catholic Biblical Encyclopedia* (New York: Joseph F. Wagner, Inc., 1956), p. 439.

2. Her story comes to us through the Deuteronomistic source. The term "Deuteronomic" is used to describe the literary style or theological content of Deuteronomy, while the term "Deuteronomistic" refers to the writer or editor of a Deuteronomic body of source material.

3. In its present context the interest of the author is in Rahab's profession of faith. See John A. Grindel, C.M., "Joshua" in *The Collegeville Bible Commentary* (Collegeville, Minn.: Liturgical Press, 1989), p. 233.

4. Gerhard Von Rad, *El Libro del Genesis* (Salamanca, Spain: Sigueme, 1977), p. 239.

5. See Steinmueller and Sullivan, p. 439.

6. Houses built into the city wall or which used the city wall for their own inner walls have been found at ancient sites. Archeological digs also revealed that the upper stories of these houses were higher than the city wall. It was through the window of such a house that Paul escaped from Damascus. Cf. Acts 9:25; 2 Cor. 11:33. See commentary of *The New American Bible*, p. 206.

7. James B. Pritchard, ed., *Ancient Near East: Anthology of Texts and Pictures*, Volume 1 (Princeton, N.J.: Princeton University Press, 1973), pp. 149–50.

8. See Boadt, p. 213. However, other Scripture scholars contend that the origin and etymology of "Canaan" remain obscure. It is ɔly a Semitic term, but the effort to link Canaan with the

Akkadian word *kinahhu*, referring to the redness of a wool dye, is problematic. See Paul J. Achtemeier, gen. ed., *Harpers Bible Dictionary* (San Francisco: Harper and Row, 1985), p. 151.

9. See Boadt, p. 213.

10. See Deut. 20:16–18.

11. See Grindel, p. 236.

12. Edith Deen, *All the Women of the Bible* (San Francisco: Harper and Row Publishers, 1988), p. 66.

13. According to a later Jewish legend, Rahab was one of the four most beautiful women in history. She became a righteous convert, married Joshua, and was the ancestor of eight prophets (including Jeremiah) and of Huldah the prophetess (cf. 15a). See Achtemeier, pp. 850–51.

14. Xavier Leon-Dufour, gen. ed., *Dictionary of Biblical Theology*, Updated Second Edition (Manila, Philippines: St. Paul Publications, 1990), p. 174.

15. *Ibid.*

16. *Ibid.*

17. *Ibid.*

18. *Ibid.*

19. The prophet Isaiah sees "fear of God" as one of the gifts of the Spirit of God (Isa. 11:2); sages speak of it as the beginning of wisdom (Prov. 1:7; Ps. 111:10); and Ben Sira shows it as practically equivalent to piety (Sir. 1:11–20). See *Dictionary of Biblical Theology*, p. 175.

20. See Deen, p. 67.

21. See *CCB* commentary, p. 137. The same theme is echoed in John's accounts about the Samaritan woman (John 4:4–42) and the adulteress (John 8:1–11). However, according to theologian Marie-Eloise Rosenblatt, R.S.M., women who are learning to re-read the Scriptures from a feminist perspective are resisting a description of their relationship to Jesus which rests only on their status as forgiven sinners. For instance, in the case of the Samaritan woman the usual interpretation in sermons identifies her as a sinner, a prostitute. Yet Jesus never mentions "sin" or "forgiveness." "The fact that she has had five husbands means many other things than a count of her adulteries." The men may have abused, divorced, or abandoned her. Cf. Marie-Eloise Rosenblatt, R.S.M., "A New Look at Scripture through Women's Eyes" in *The Catholic World*, November-December 1991.

22. See Kamol Arayaprateep, "Christ in the Concrete Life Situation in Thailand," *Asian Women Doing Theology: Report from Singapore Conference, November 20–29, 1987* (Hong Kong: Asian Women's Resource Centre for Culture and Theology, 1989), pp. 90–91.

23. See *Womenews*, April-June 1991. This report on women prostitutes in Olongapo City in the Philippines is based on an article that appeared in this issue.

24. There are approximately 100,000 Filipinos in Japan, of whom 90 percent are women. Out of this 90 percent, no less than 80 percent are working as nightclub hostesses or receptionists in small bars and cocktail lounges in the districts of Shinjuku, Roppongi, Akasaka, and elsewhere in Tokyo. See *Bakud*, vol. 1, no. 1, August 1991.

25. Adel Hijos, "Mamac Case in Focus" in *Womenews*, January-March 1991 issue, p. 10. A follow-up report by the same author appeared in the April-June 1991 issue of the same newsletter.

26. *Ibid.*

27. *Ibid.*

3. JEPHTHAH'S DAUGHTER

1. Gerda Lerner, *The Creation of Patriarchy, Women and History* (New York and Oxford: Oxford University Press, 1986), p. 173. Cited by Sharon Pace Jeansonne, *The Women of Genesis: From Sarah to Potiphar's Wife* (Minneapolis: Fortress Press, 1990), p. 36.

2. Edith Deen, *All of the Women of the Bible* (San Francisco: Harper & Row, Publishers, 1983), p. 307.

3. John A. Grindel, "Joshua, Judges" in *The Collegeville Bible Commentary* (Collegeville, Minn.: Liturgical Press, 1989), p. 248.

4. Lawrence Boadt, *Reading the Old Testament: An Introduction* (New York/Mahwah, N.J.: Paulist Press, 1984), p. 207.

5. See footnote, *The Oxford Annotated Bible with the Apocrypha, Revised Standard Version*, ed. Herbert G. May and Bruce M. Metzger (New York: Oxford University Press, 1965), p. 308.

6. By *the Spirit*, people in those times meant the superhuman strength Yahweh gives to any person to accomplish extraordinary feats like winning wars.

7. Jephthah's vow and its fulfillment show the primitive character of his religion and that of his contemporaries, who retain this story as an example of genuine devotion. Cf. John L. McKenzie, S.J., *Dictionary of the Bible* (New York: Macmillan Publishing Co., Inc. and London: Collier Macmillan Publishing, 1975), p. 419.

8. This can clearly be gleaned from the account of Abraham's sacrifice of Isaac. As early as that time the Israelites looked upon human sacrifice with horror. The story of Isaac certainly shows how Yahweh forbade this practice. Yahweh did not want human flesh but would

accept animals as an offering instead, although Yahweh most wanted faith and trust. See Boadt, p. 143. According to Scripture scholars, there are a number of parallels to this event in comparative folklore. See Grindel, pp. 258–59.

9. See comments in *The Catholic Study Bible, The New American Bible* (New York/Oxford: Oxford University Press, 1990), p. RG 131.

10. See Phyllis Trible, *Texts of Terror: Literary-Feminist Readings of Biblical Narratives* (Philadelphia: Fortress Press, 1984), p. 96.

11. *Ibid.*

12. "A comparable sacrifice is Agamemnon's offering of his daughter Iphigenia in order to obtain fair winds for the Greek fleet bound for Troy." Cf. *The New Jerome Biblical Commentary* (Englewood Cliffs, N.J.: Prentice Hall, 1990), p. 141.

13. Such a celebration is part of the tradition of the Israelite people. Long ago, after God brought back the water of the sea upon Pharaoh and his chariots, Miriam the prophetess "took a timbrel in her hand; and all the women went out after her with music and dancing" (Exod. 15:18–21). The same tradition is practiced even after many centuries. In David's time, when he returned from slaying the Philistines, the women came out of all the cities of Israel, singing and dancing to meet King Saul and David (1 Sam. 18:5–7).

14. See Trible, p. 100.

15. *Ibid.*, p. 102.

16. Xavier Leon-Dufour, ed., *Dictionary of Biblical Theology*, Updated Second Edition (Manila, Philippines: St. Paul Publications, 1990), p. 513.

17. See Trible, p. 102.

18. See *The Catholic Study Bible*, p. RG 131.

19. See Trible, p. 105.

20. Cf. Ps. 128:3–6.

21. The First Book of Samuel proclaims his military prowess (1 Sam. 12:11). Jephthah's name, though not specifically mentioned, is inferred in Sir. 46:11–12.

22. See Leon-Dufour, p. 513. According to Old Testament theology, blood plays a large role in the idea of atonement, but its efficacy is ultimately derived from the divine will (Lev. 17:11) and supposes sentiments of repentance.

23. According to biblical scholars, "it is difficult to know how the Deuteronomistic writers intended this story to be viewed in context for there is no comment at all on the actions of the main characters." Cf. *The Catholic Study Bible*, p. RG 131.

24. See Trible, p. 108.

25. See Leon-Dufour, p. 514.

26. Judette A. Gallares, r.c., *Following God's Call* (Quezon City, Philippines: Claretian Publications, 1990), p. 37.

27. Scripture scholars contend that the greater horror in the texts is not the human sacrifice, which functioned as an acceptable cultic practice, but the fact that Jephthah's daughter is his only child and because of this sacrifice he will have no future progeny. See commentary of *The Catholic Study Bible*, p. RG 131.

28. Henri Nouwen, *Reaching Out* (Garden City, N.Y.: Doubleday, 1975), pp. 22–23.

29. Demetrius Dumm, O.S.B., *Flowers in the Desert: A Spirituality of the Bible* (New York/Mahwah, N.J.: Paulist Press, 1987), p. 143. Citing Nouwen's distinction between loneliness and solitude.

30. Judette A. Gallares, *Praying with Job* (Quezon City, Philippines: Claretian Publications, 1991), p. 15.

31. *Ibid.*, p. 14.

32. *Church Trends*, no. 2, 1990–91 (Quezon City, Philippines: Church Data Center), p. 6.

33. "Amnesty International Reports on Human Rights Violations Against Fairer Sex" in the *Philippine Daily Inquirer*, 7 March 1991, as quoted in *Church Trends*, p. 17.

34. Ann Wansbrough, *Liturgy* in the Domestic Violence Resource Package Commission of the Status of Women (Australian Council of Churches, 1986), as quoted in the *Asian Women Doing Theology* (Hong Kong: Asian Women's Resource Centre for Culture and Theology, 1989), p. 148.

4. RUTH AND NAOMI

1. John L. McKenzie, S.J., *Dictionary of the Bible* (New York: Macmillan Publishing Co., Inc. and London: Collier Macmillan Publishers, 1975), p. 927.

2. *Ibid.*

3. *Ibid.*

4. Most scholars find it difficult to date the Book of Ruth with any certainty. Pauline Viviano comments that some argue for its postexilic origin, while more seem to advance the preexilic period argument. Those who postulate a postexilic date see the book as a polemical work challenging the policies of Ezra forbidding intermarriage with foreign women. The book questions such a policy by showing that Ruth, though a foreign woman, is pious and faithful to Israel's covenant. The book's

ending, which links Ruth and David by blood, is a clear challenge to Ezra's policies. On the other hand, those who argue for the preexilic date base their argument on the analysis of the book's style and theology. "There is nothing in the style of the book that would force one to assume a late date. The book's theology is similar to that of the Joseph story (Gen. 37-50) and the court history of David (2 Sam. 9-20), both thought to be preexilic in origin." Cf. Pauline A. Viviano, "Ruth Reading Guide" in *The Catholic Study Bible, The New American Bible* (New York/Oxford: Oxford University Press, 1990), pp. RG 141-46.

5. Alice L. Laffey, "Ruth," *The New Jerome Biblical Commentary* (Englewood Cliffs, N.J.: Prentice Hall, 1990), p. 553.

6. See Viviano, p. RG 141.

7. *Ibid.*

8. The levirate law is mentioned in Genesis 38. Here it is indicated that when a man dies without leaving children, the sacred duty of his widow is to marry the nearest relative of her deceased husband. The first son she would have from him would bear the name of the dead man and would be considered his son.

9. Scripture scholars contend that these verses from Deuteronomy reflect later problems with the Moabites legitimized by reference to Israel's past and their historical entrance into the land, whereas Ruth represents an earlier period when the Moabites were merely Israel's neighbors (Gerleman). Cf. Laffey, *The New Jerome Biblical Commentary,* p. 555.

10. *Ibid.*

11. Intermarriage was prohibited not on ethnic grounds but to avoid religious syncretism and to foster the worship of Yahweh (cf. Exod. 34:15ff.). See Madeleine S. Miller and J. Lane Miller, *Harper's Bible Dictionary* (New York, Hagerstown, San Francisco, London: Harper and Row Publishers, 1973), p. 422.

12. *Ibid.*

13. *Ibid.*

14. See Viviano, p. RG 143.

15. See Laffey, p. 555.

16. *Ibid.*

17. Edith Deen, *All of the Women of the Bible* (San Francisco: Harper and Row Publishers, 1983), p. 84.

18. James A. Fischer, C.M., "Ruth," *The Collegeville Bible Commentary* (Collegeville, Minn.: Liturgical Press, 1989), p. 798. Complaining to and blaming God belongs to the prayer of lament. As in Job, the conflict between Naomi and Yahweh is open and absolute.

19. See Laffey, p. 556.

20. See Viviano, p. RG 144.

21. See Laffey, p. 556.

22. See Fischer, p. 800.

23. *Ibid.*

24. See Laffey, p. 556. The article cites the contributions of E. F. Campbell, Jr., *Ruth* (AB 7; GC, 1975) and P. Humbert, "Art et leçon de l'histoire de Ruth," *RTP* 26 (1939), pp. 257-86.

25. See Viviano, p. RG 145.

26. See Laffey, p. 556.

27. See Fischer, p. 801. Laffey also mentions that many commentators (Craghan, Murphy, Rauber) believe the author is pointing back to Yahweh's wings, in which case Yahweh's protective wings are being symbolically transferred to Boaz's skirt. Cf. Laffey, p. 557.

28. See Laffey, p. 557.

29. See Fischer, p. 801.

30. *Ibid.,* p. 802.

31. See Laffey, p. 557.

32. See Fischer, p. 802.

33. See Laffey, p. 554. The author cites two sources: H. J. Boecker, *Law and the Administration of Justice in the Old Testament and the Ancient East* (Minneapolis, Minn.: Augsburg, 1980) and A. Gordis, "Love, Marriage, and Business in the Book of Ruth," *A Light Unto My Path* (*Festschrift* for J. M. Myers, ed. H. N. Bream, et al., Philadelphia, 1974), pp. 241-64.

34. Raymond E. Brown, *A Coming Christ in Advent: Essays on the Gospel Narratives Preparing for the Birth of Jesus* (Collegeville, Minn.: Liturgical Press, 1988), p. 24. Reprinted by Claretian Publications for distribution in the Philippines, India, and Pakistan by license of the Liturgical Press.

35. See Fischer, p. 802.

36. See Viviano, p. RG 145.

37. See Laffey, p. 557.

38. *Ibid.*

39. See Fischer, p. 803.

40. The corresponding list that appears in 1 Chronicles 2 does not include her either.

41. See Brown, p. 24.

42. Quoted by Joyce Rupp, O.S.M., in *Praying Our Goodbyes* (Notre Dame, Ind.: Ave Maria Press, 1988), p. 77.

43. *Ibid.,* p. 24.

44. John Steinmueller ánd Kathryn Sullivan, eds., *Catholic Biblical*

Encyclopedia (New York: Joseph Wagner, Inc. Publishers, 1956), pp. 176-77.

45. Xavier Leon-Dufour, gen. ed., *Dictionary of Biblical Theology,* Updated Second Edition (Manila, Philippines: St. Paul Publications, 1990), pp. 48-49.

46. Emphasis mine.

47. See Laffey, p. 554, citing for her source A. Gordis, "Love, Marriage and Business in the Book of Ruth," *A Light Unto My Path,* pp. 241-64.

48. See footnote commentary in the *Christian Community Bible,* Fourth Edition (Quezon City, Philippines: Claretian Publications, St. Paul Publications, Divine Word Publications, 1990), p. 57.

49. The title of the prayer is mine. Taken from an untitled prayer. See "Women in Australia," *Asian Women Doing Theology,* Report from Singapore Conference (Kowloon, Hong Kong: Asian Women's Resource Centre for Culture and Theology, 1989), pp. 149-50. Quoted from Ann Wansbrough, *Liturgy,* in Domestic Violence Resource Package, Commission of the Status of Women, Australian Council of Churches, 1986.

5. ABIGAIL

1. The Deuteronomic books include Deuteronomy, Joshua, Judges, 1 and 2 Samuel, and 1 and 2 Kings.

2. Xavier Leon-Dufour, gen. ed., *Dictionary of Biblical Theology,* Updated Second Edition (Manila, Philippines: St. Paul Publications, 1990), p. 640.

3. *Ibid.*

4. *Ibid.*

5. Brother John of Taizé, *The Pilgrim God: A Biblical Journey* (Washington, D.C.: The Pastoral Press, 1985), p. 33.

6. *Ibid.*

7. It becomes an historical fact that in the course of the centuries since Israel's occupation of Canaan, Israel has experienced a life of combat in which the national dynamism is placed in the service of a religious cause, such as offensive wars against Sihon and Og (Num. 21:21-35; Deut. 2:26-3:17), Joshua's conquest of Canaan (Josh. 6-12), defensive wars against Midian (Num. 31), and so on.

8. See Brother John of Taizé, p. 33.

9. Cf. Gen. 38:13; 2 Sam. 13:23 ff.

10. Paula J. Bowes, "1 and 2 Samuel" in *The Collegeville Bible Com-*

mentary (Collegeville, Minn.: The Liturgical Press, 1989), p. 280.

11. Charles Conroy, M.S.C., *1-2 Samuel, 1-2 Kings* (Wilmington, Del.: Michael Glazier, Inc., 1983), p. 80.

12. See Bowes, p. 280.

13. *Ibid.*

14. *Ibid.*

15. *Dictionary of Biblical Theology,* pp. 626-627.

16. *Ibid.*

17. *Ibid.*

18. See Bowes, p. 280.

19. See Leon-Dufour, p. 626.

20. David gives in to vengeance on Shimei and Joab (1 Kings 2:6-46). At any rate, the duty to obey the "law of holiness" is limited to brothers of the one race. Cf. Leon-Dufour, p. 626.

21. See Bowes, p. 280.

22. *Ibid.*

23. Abraham sends his servant Eliezer to Nahor to find a wife for his son, Isaac. Eliezer does the proposing in the name of Abraham for his son (cf. Gen. 24).

24. Abigail is one of David's eight wives. The others were Michal (1 Sam. 18:27), Bathsheba (2 Sam. 12:24), Ahinoam, Maacah, Haggith, Abital, and Eglah (2 Sam. 2-5). In Israel polygamy belonged to the permitted exceptions, at least in the Old Testament. It was due to political considerations (such as among the kings) or to prestige and "status." It was often connected to childlessness, in which case the husband "received" or "took" a concubine (Gen. 16:1-4; 30:1-13; 1 Sam. 1:2). See A. S. Van Der Woude, gen. ed., *The World of the Bible* (Grand Rapids, Mich.: Wm. B. Eerdmans Publishing Co., 1986), p. 351.

25. See Bowes, p. 280.

26. *Womenews,* vol. VIII, no. 26, p. 2.

6. TWO UNNAMED WOMEN

1. Bathsheba was one of David's wives (2 Samuel 11). The queen of Sheba visited Solomon after hearing of his wisdom and fame in order to test him with difficult questions (1 Kings 10).

2. Gwilym H. Jones, *1 & 2 Kings, The New Century Bible Commentary* (Grand Rapids, Mich.: Wm. B. Eerdmans Publishing Co./London: Marshall, Morgan and Scott Publishing Ltd., 1948). Jones cites in his commentary that a valid distinction is drawn between narratives and anecdotes (cf. Schmitt in *Elisha,* pp. 89ff.). Based on Schmitt's more

detailed analysis, he traces three stages in the development of the narrative: (i) At the latter end of the process, a narrative that lacked any theological interest whatsoever was theologized by means of three short additions. The reference in v. 33b to Elisha's prayer to the Lord has introduced a new element to the semimagical practice of vv. 33-35. (ii) The original narrative has been later revised by the redactor of the wonder narratives collection but with many modifications. (iii) Since vv. 17b and 32 have been designated as later additions, the only remaining reference to Elisha is found in v. 8; elsewhere he is called "the man of God." This would suggest that originally this was a narrative about an unnamed "man of God," who was later identified with Elisha by the addition of his name.

3. John L. McKenzie, S.J., *Dictionary of the Bible* (New York: Macmillan Publishing Co. & London: Collier Macmillan Publishing Co., 1965), p. 579.

4. *Ibid.*

5. *Ibid.*

6. *Ibid.,* p. 578.

7. *Ibid.*

8. *Ibid.,* p. 579.

9. Charles Conroy, M.S.C., *1-2 Samuel, 1-2 Kings* (Wilmington, Del.: Michael Glazier, Inc., 1983), p. 179.

10. *Ibid.*

11. Patrick L. Ryan, "Giving Your All" in *America,* November 2, 1991, p. 327.

12. See Jones, p. 306.

13. Although the text does not specifically mention Elijah's clothing, prophets were known at that time through the mantle they wore over their heads.

14. Edith Deen, *All of the Women in the Bible* (San Francisco: Harper & Row, Publishers, 1983), p. 351.

15. See Conroy, p. 178.

16. The prophet's location at this time can be misleading if we have to rely only on v. 25. Jones admits that there is no evidence of a group of prophets in Carmel, only a man of God operating on his own. The connection between vv. 1-7 and both the anecdotes in vv. 38-41 and 6:1-7 indicate that they originated from the prophetic group in Gilgal. See Jones, p. 403.

17. See Deen, p. 351.

18. Cf. Hammurabi Code 117. James B. Pritchard, ed., *The Ancient Near East, An Anthology of Texts and Pictures,* vol. 1 (Princeton, N.J.: Princeton University Press, 1993), p. 151.

19. The Christian Community Bible specifically says "a little oil for cleaning." However, several translations of the Bible simply say "a pot of oil" (JB) or "a jar of oil" (RSV).

20. Colomban Lesquivit, O.S.B., and Marc-François Lacan, O.S.B., "Oil" in *Dictionary of Biblical Theology,* Updated Second Edition, Xavier Leon-Dufour, gen. ed. (Manila, Philippines: St. Paul Publications, 1990), pp. 398-99.

21. Madeleine S. and J. Lane Miller, *The New Harper's Bible Dictionary* (New York, Hagerstown, San Francisco, London: Harper & Row, Publishers, 1973), p. 501.

22. Paul Ternant, P.B., "Miracles" in *Dictionary of Biblical Theology,* pp. 361-62.

23. "Fear of God" in Old Testament spirituality is a virtue. It means the awe and reverence one must have for God (Prov. 5:7; Eccles. 12:13). That is why the Scripture writers say that "fear of the Lord is the beginning of wisdom." This "fear of the Lord" is represented by the "fear and trembling" with which Paul exhorted the Philippians to work out their salvation (Phil. 2:12).

24. See Ryan, p. 327.

25. Bruce J. Malina, "Hospitality" in *Harper's Bible Dictionary* (San Francisco: Harper & Row Publishers, 1985), p. 408.

26. *Ibid.*

27. See Miller, p. 270.

28. *Ibid.*

29. For example, the story of Jael (Judg. 4:17-24), who received Sisera (the commander of Israel's enemy) hospitably and provided him his needs. But when he was fast asleep, Jael took a workman's hammer and a long tent peg and drove it through Sisera's temple.

30. Brother John of Taizé, *The Pilgrim God: A Biblical Journey* (Washington, D.C.: The Pastoral Press, 1985), p. 200.

31. Pierre-Marie Galopin, O.S.B., and Marc-François Lacan, O.S.B., "Hospitality" in *Dictionary of Biblical Theology,* p. 243.

7. MIRIAM

1. Edith Deen, *All of the Women in the Bible* (San Francisco: Harper & Row, Publishers, 1983), p. 58.

2. Irene Nowell, O.S.B., "Roles of Women in the Old Testament," *The Bible Today,* vol. 28, no. 8, November 1990, p. 364.

3. See Deen, p. 59.

4. See Nowell, p. 365.

5. J.P. Hyatt, "Exodus," *The New Century Bible Commentary* (Grand Rapids, Mich.: Wm. B. Eerdmans Publishing Co.; London: Marshall, Morgan & Scott Publishing, Ltd., 1984), p. 162.

6. *Ibid.* The author refers to the opinion of Cross and Freedman.

7. The language has been adapted to make it more inclusive.

8. DEBORAH

1. Edith Deen, *All of the Women in the Bible* (San Francisco: Harper & Row, Publishers, 1983), p. 69.

2. Irene Nowell, O.S.B., "Roles of Women in the Old Testament," *The Bible Today,* vol. 28, no. 8, November 1990, p. 365.

3. Paul Achtemeier, gen. ed., *Harper's Bible Dictionary* (San Francisco: Harper & Row, 1985), p. 214. Modern critics and biblical scholars are unanimous in affirming the antiquity of this poem. However, many of them believe that the traditional attribution is not enough of itself to establish the authorship of Deborah. Cf. John L. McKenzie, S.J., *Dictionary of the Bible* (New York: Macmillan Publishing Co./London: Collier Macmillan Publishers, 1975), p. 185.

4. M. O'Connor, "Judges" in *The New Jerome Biblical Commentary.*

5. *Ibid.*

6. See *Harper's Bible Dictionary.*

7. The language has been adapted to make it more inclusive.

9. HANNAH

1. Paul Achtemeier, gen. ed., *Harper's Bible Dictionary* (San Francisco: Harper & Row, 1985), pp. 372-73. For similar passages in Wisdom literature, see Ps. 113:5-9; Job 12:7-25; Eccles. 10:5-7.

2. John L. McKenzie, S.J., *Dictionary of the Bible* (New York: Macmillan Publishing Co./London: Collier Macmillan Publishers, 1975), p. 337.

3. The language has been adapted to make it more inclusive.

10. JUDITH

1. This is an unusual instance in the Old Testament where a woman had rights over her own property and acted with great independence in disposing them.

2. See "Judith Reading Guide" in *The Catholic Study Bible, The New American Bible* (New York/Oxford: Oxford University Press, 1990), p. RG 212.

3. *Ibid.*

4. John L. McKenzie, S.J., *Dictionary of the Bible* (New York: Macmillan Publishing Co./London: Collier Macmillan Publishers, 1975), p. 469.

5. *Ibid.* The author is careful to state that Judith did not have to complete her seduction of Holofernes before she could kill him (13:16). Like earlier stories, the Book of Judith shows that God does bring deliverance out of the evil that people create for themselves. See also "Judith Reading Guide," p. RG 214.

6. *Ibid.*

7. *The New Jerome Biblical Commentary,* p. 575.

8. The language has been adapted to make it more inclusive.

11. ESTHER

1. Jews in exile frequently bore a Jewish and a foreign name. See *The New Jerome Biblical Commentary* (Englewood Cliffs, N.J.: Prentice Hall, 1990), p. 577.

2. The Book of Esther has a shorter Hebrew version and a Greek version with several additions which the Hebrews and the Protestants do not accept as canonical. See "Reading Guide" in *The Catholic Study Bible, The New American Bible* (New York/Oxford: Oxford University Press, 1990), p. RG 215.

3. Esther's story is a novella on the theme of the persecuted righteous and their deliverance. The story does have a historical "flavor," but it does not intend to report an actual event. See "Esther Reading Guide," p. RG 217.

4. Unconsciously Esther participates in the process to replace Vashti, who is the real heroine in this story, according to the feminist reading of the text. See "Esther Reading Guide," p. RG 217.

5. This seems to be what the author wanted the readers to conclude.

6. The Bible does not mention this feast anywhere else except in 2 Macc. 15:36 as an allusion to "Mordecai's Day." Even though the Hebrew version of the book makes no reference to God, celebration of Mordecai's victory as a religious feast makes it clear that the victory came from God. See "Esther Reading Guide," pp. RG 215-18.

7. See *The New Jerome Biblical Commentary,* p. 578.

8. The language has been adapted to make it more inclusive.

12. SUSANNA

1. Considered an addition to Daniel in the Greek translation of the Hebrew Old Testament. Like the additions in the Book of Esther, neither the Hebrew nor the Protestant Bible accepts the appendages as canonical.

2. Xavier Leon-Dufour, gen. ed., "Confidence" in *Dictionary of Biblical Theology,* Updated Second Edition (Manila, Philippines: St. Paul Publications, 1990), p. 89.

CONCLUSION

1. Part of talk on feminist theology given by James Reise, S.J., on 24 July 1993 at the Loyola School of Theology, Philippines.

2. This was part of a lecture given by Dr. Carolyn Jacobs on 20 June 1993 to a group of Cenacle sisters preparing for final vows at the Cenacle Retreat House in Lake Ronkonkoma, Long Island, New York.

3. Adapted from the insights of Dr. Jacobs.

4. Based on a lecture on "Communication" given at the East Asian Pastoral Institute by Ibarra Gonzalez, S.J., on 25 May 1993.